Reimagining the Role of Teachers in Nature-based Learning

Learn how to integrate nature-based pedagogy in this practical and inviting book. Nature-based teaching is getting more attention in early childhood education settings and can positively impact the development of young children's curiosity, confidence, and care. You'll learn to not only identify but also embody the many roles teachers play when implementing nature-based strategies. Chapters lay out the research and theory behind each role, specific language or behaviors of what that role looks like in practice, and reflexive questions to help educators reflect on their practice. This is perfect for in-service early childhood educators, including infant, toddler, preschool, and elementary providers, interested in more intentional use of nature in their teaching.

Dr. Rachel A. Larimore is an educational consultant, speaker, researcher, and author of four previous books. Her work focuses on the intentional integration of nature to support young children's holistic development by learning with nature to expand their worlds and live rich, full lives.

Dr. Claire H. Warden is an educational entrepreneur, researcher, and author of more than 10 books including her most recent, *Green Teaching: Nature Pedagogies for Climate Change and Sustainability*.

T0384974

Other Eye on Education Books
Available from Routledge
(www.routledge.com/eyeoneducation)

This is Homeschooling
Stories of Unconventional Learning Practices
On the Road and In Nature
Karie Rybakova Mathews

A Practical Guide to Leading Green Schools
Partnering with Nature to Create Vibrant, Flourishing,
Sustainable Schools
Cynthia L. Uline and Lisa A. W. Kensler

Place-Based Scientific Inquiry
A Practical Handbook for Teaching Outside
Benjamin Wong Blonder, Ja'Nya Banks, Austin Cruz, Anna Dornhaus,
R. Keating Godfrey, Joshua S. Hoskinson, Rebecca Lipson,
Pacifica Sommers, Christy Stewart, and Alan Strauss

The Kinderchat Guide to Elementary School Projects
A Playful Approach to Learning
Heidi Echternacht

Reimagining the Role of Teachers in Nature-based Learning

Helping Children be Curious, Confident, and Caring

Rachel A. Larimore and Claire H. Warden

Routledge
Taylor & Francis Group

NEW YORK AND LONDON

Designed cover image: © Getty Images

First published 2025
by Routledge
605 Third Avenue, New York, NY 10158

and by Routledge
4 Park Square, Milton Park, Abingdon, Oxon, OX14 4RN

Routledge is an imprint of the Taylor & Francis Group, an informa business

© 2025 Taylor & Francis

Library of Congress Cataloging-in-Publication Data
Names: Larimore, Rachel, author. | Warden, Claire, author.
Title: Reimagining the role of teachers in nature-based learning : helping children be curious, confident, and caring / Rachel A. Larimore and Claire H. Warden.
Description: New York, NY : Routledge, 2024. | Series: Eye on education | Includes bibliographical references.
Identifiers: LCCN 2024014271 | ISBN 9781032448206 (hardback) | ISBN 9781032399409 (paperback) | ISBN 9781003374053 (ebook)
Subjects: LCSH: Science--Study and teaching (Early childhood) | Nature study. | Environmental education. | Outdoor education. | Curiosity in children. | Confidence in children. | Caring in children.
Classification: LCC LB1139.5.S35 L368 2024 | DDC 372.35/7044--dc23/eng/20240611
LC record available at https://lccn.loc.gov/2024014271

ISBN: 978-1-032-44820-6 (hbk)
ISBN: 978-1-032-39940-9 (pbk)
ISBN: 978-1-003-37405-3 (ebk)

DOI: 10.4324/9781003374053

Typeset in Palatino
by SPi Technologies India Pvt Ltd (Straive)

Contents

Preface

When you travel, your path will cross with many people. Every now and again, you meet someone who just makes you feel understood, as if you have known them for years and it has only been a few days. That was our experience and what led to a wonderful personal and professional friendship and eventually this book. While we technically met in 2006, it wasn't until 2015 that we had the opportunity to spend extended time together. By 2019, we had spent lots of time together, on both sides of the Atlantic Ocean, and knew we needed to write a book together.

One of the many things that led to our sense of belonging with one another is that we both believe in the power of relationships and that relationships are the root of co-constructivism—a theory of learning we both operate from. Thus, it seemed only natural to write a book that explores those different types of relationships—in particular, the roles that we believe make a difference in the lives of children. We both strongly believe children deserve to be surrounded by adults who are respectful, caring, and interested in what they think, say, do, and make.

We also both believe that children have a right to a relationship with the natural world. Over our long careers working with young children in nature-based spaces, we are convinced they have a special relationship with nature that we can learn from. This feeling has been reinforced by our extensive interactions with practitioners as well as our doctoral research. Claire's research explored the creation and theorization of nature pedagogy. Rachel's explored teacher–child interactions in programs that did and did not use nature pedagogy.

Through these experiences and research, we have noticed the power of curiosity, care, and confidence as the foundational ideas that emerge from children's relationships with ourselves, others, and the natural world. We've seen the positive ways curiosity, care, and confidence emerge. We've also seen what happens when they are not supported. This book seeks to support adults to feel the impact they have every time they interact with a child irrespective of where they work.

We hope this book affirms and celebrates the amazing work early childhood educators are already doing. We also hope it encourages educators to embrace an attitude of self-improvement to ensure quality in our practice so that we provide young children with the childhoods they deserve. We hope the blend of both practical and theoretical perspectives of the various adult roles will allow for tangible actions alongside an understanding of why those actions matter.

This book is aimed to be useful to everyone, but it is influenced by our advocacy to embrace nature pedagogy as a way of teaching and learning Inside, Outside, and Beyond.

Claire Warden (Scotland) &
Rachel Larimore (United States)
January 2024

Acknowledgments

We are social constructivists who believe learning happens through interactions with others. That includes us as authors. We want to acknowledge the many people who have contributed to our journey to the publication of this book. The numerous conversations and experiences through our professional work and our own childhoods have led to this moment.

We are incredibly grateful for the many educators around the globe who have invited us in our role as consultants into their settings, classrooms, and professional learning journey. We always receive as much or more from our interactions than we are able to give. Each interaction helps us reflect, refine, and clarify our perspectives on nature pedagogy.

Another group of educators that has helped shape our journey to this book are the many teachers we have worked with in our roles as directors at Auchlone Nature Kindergarten in Scotland (Claire) and Chippewa Nature Center's Nature Preschool in the United States (Rachel). In these spaces, our day-to-day interactions with children and teachers helped sculpt our perspectives on nature-based pedagogy in order to facilitate children's learning *with* nature. I would like to acknowledge Morrison's Academy. Crieff. Scotland, UK for the image of adult and child in Figure 6.1.

Throughout the book, we talk about the importance of individual, personal work related to the attitudes and actions we bring to our work as educators. This work begins very early and continues throughout our lives. With that in mind, we want to acknowledge the influence of our friends and family on creating the educators we are today. For both of us, this started young with extensive time playing outdoors and the guidance and support of loving adults. This undoubtedly contributed to our perspectives as nature pedagogues.

Again, thank you to everyone we have spent moments and had conversations with over the years. Our journeys have been enriched by every one. We hope the words in this book will spark even more conversations in the future.

Meet the authors

Rachel A. Larimore, PhD
Dr. Rachel A. Larimore is an educational consultant, speaker, researcher, and author. Her work focuses on the intentional integration of nature to support young children's holistic development by learning with nature to expand their worlds and live rich, full lives. She has written multiple books, including *Establishing a Nature-Based Preschool*, *Preschool Beyond Walls: Blending Early Childhood Education and Nature-Based Learning*, and *Evaluating Nature: Evaluating Natureness: Measuring the Quality of Nature-based Classrooms in Pre-K Through 3rd Grade*. Rachel is the founder and chief visionary of Samara Early Learning, an organization focused on helping early childhood educators start nature-based schools or add nature-based approaches into their existing program. Prior to founding Samara, she spent more than a decade starting and directing one of the first nature-based preschools in the United States.

Claire H. Warden, PhD
Dr. Claire Warden is an educational entrepreneur, researcher, and author of more than 10 books, including her most recent *Green Teaching: Nature Pedagogies for Climate Change and Sustainability*. Claire shares her wisdom and thinking through her prolific writing and online through Mindstretchers Academy, which is based in Scotland. Her work around planning with and for children through Floorbooks™ has earned her international recognition as a pioneer in actively standing for the rights of children to be heard in all aspects of education programming. She coaches colleagues across the world to embrace nature pedagogy to form a meshwork, metaphorically and physically, to build awareness of a way of working with children and families so that they don't just learn about nature but also learn in, for, with, and, ultimately, from the more than human relationships that surround them.

About the book

This book articulates the many roles nature-based early childhood educators play in supporting young children to become more curious, confident, and caring. The nature-based education movement continues to grow globally and we're living in a high-stress, post-pandemic world. This book is intended to provide insights for educators who are currently using nature-based pedagogy in their early years classrooms or would like to make shifts toward the approach in order to support children's holistic development.

Reimagining the Role of Teachers in Nature-based Learning: Helping Children be Curious, Confident, & Caring includes 11 different roles teachers play in the early childhood classroom. These roles are presented from foundational to more complex. However, the order does not indicate a level of importance. All of these roles are important in the early childhood classroom. Each has its own impact and potential trade-offs, but each of these different adult roles help create a rich, holistic learning environment for young children. Each chapter provides an overview of the role, why it is important for young children's learning, and how we can intentionally implement the role. At the end of each chapter, we've provided examples of language you might hear in the Inside, Outside, or Beyond classrooms as evidence of the adult role. There are also self-reflection questions to help teachers explore how the ideas discussed in the book play out in practice. The final chapter of the book is an invitation to educators to more deeply explore the individual values, attitudes, and beliefs they bring to interactions with young children.

The book serves as a catalyst for reflection about the important role educators play in day-to-day interactions with the young children they care for. It is a useful reading for in-service and pre-service practitioners, researchers, and policymakers about the social-emotional aspects of teaching in the early years.

1

Introduction

The world is on fire—both literally and figuratively. In fact, as a result of global climate change, today's children will experience twice as many droughts and wildfires and three times more river floods and crop failures in their lifetime as someone who is 60 today (Thiery et al., 2021). If that isn't disheartening enough, the same study found children born today will experience an average of 30 extreme heat waves in their lifetime–this is seven times that of today's 60-year-olds.

In addition to global climate change, there are many conflicts happening throughout the world. According to the U.S. Council on Foreign Relations, there are 27 active conflicts throughout the world at the time of this writing. We're writing this book while two other crises are also underway—the COVID-19 pandemic and the childcare crisis.

For some, it's tempting to pretend that these current crises don't exist or that they don't impact children. However, putting our heads in the sand won't solve these problems. In fact, ignoring the realities of our world will put even more pressure on our children. Young children didn't cause any of our current global problems, but the fact is that they will inherit them. Not only will children inherit these problems, but they're already being impacted by them—at this very moment!

So often when it comes to young children, we talk about the future—being ready for kindergarten, having success in college, landing good jobs, and so on. Yet young children are humans

DOI: 10.4324/9781003374053-1

right now. They have thoughts, emotions, and physical needs. They have the right, as they are today, to express themselves, think freely, enjoy good health, play, and develop their own talents and strengths (UNICEF, 1989).

So how do we support them now and for the future they will inherit? Many argue for an emphasis on cognitive skills such as literacy and science, technology, engineering, and math. While we agree there is value in those cognitive skills, we also believe human skills are vital. These skills are often referred to as "soft skills," but we prefer the term *human skills* as thought-leader Simon Sinek calls them. By "human skills" we mean the ability to listen well, communicate effectively, problem-solve, and care for ourselves and others. Yes, technical skills will be necessary, but those are much more easily learned than human skills. Given how quickly technology advances, those skills will also change drastically between when a child is in the early years to when they are in the workforce, voting, and so on. The skills that are *much* harder to teach later in life but just as vital to solving hard problems? Human skills. The ability to relate to one another.

Many factors led to our current crises, but it could be easily argued that the absence of or poor human skills, that is, the lack of connection to and curiosity about other people, a lack of curiosity about the world around us, and a lack of care for other individuals and the planet, were partly to blame for them. What would happen if we focused in the early years on supporting children's development of confidence, curiosity, and care? We believe the focus on these skills will lead to a world we'd want our children to live in.

Why confident, curious, and caring?

With the rapidly and ever-changing world of technology, not to mention everything else in the world, there is no way to know what skills and knowledge children will need to solve the problems of the future. Yet, we *do* know that there are some things they *must* have. That's why we believe in focusing first and foremost in early years classrooms on providing experiences that will support the development of confidence, curiosity, and care rather than rote memorization of facts.

There is a good chance, if you're reading this book, that you are well aware of the *many* social-emotional skills. So you may also be thinking, "Why those three?! Why only those three? What about all the others?" We absolutely agree there are many different emotions and social-emotional constructs worth exploring. For the purposes of this book, we're combining these constructs into three big categories—confidence, curiosity, and care. (We are affectionately calling these the "3Cs.") We see these 3Cs as ideas that include many different social-emotional constructs related to *how* we teach as well as *what* we teach. In the following subsections, we'll explain in more detail.

Confidence

Confidence is believing in one's abilities and strengths. We believe it's important for young children to have confidence in who they are and the many strengths they possess. This confidence can be developed in young children when adults treat them as though they are competent and capable, in other words when adults not only recognize but also build on the many strengths that every child inherently possesses.

Confidence is a key element to children's sense of agency, or the belief they hold about their ability to influence or change the world around them. A sense of agency is critical to an engaged citizenry that strives to solve the many crises we face as a society—rather than simply accepting them as fate. In the early childhood classroom, this confidence and sense of agency might look like children saying, "Stop! I don't like it when you push me!" or asking the teacher for different colored watercolors or the entire class voting on where they'd like to hike to that day. With the world on fire, as we mentioned earlier, it is imperative that young children have the confidence to influence their world not only while they're young but also when they are able to vote and join the workforce.

One definition of *confidence* is "the quality or state of being certain." While confidence has many positives, there is also a danger in certainty. Thus, we're not implying that we want to encourage arrogance. Rather, we are suggesting confident humility. *Confident humility* is having faith in our abilities while at the same time being open to the notion that we may not have the right answers—let alone be addressing the right problem (Grant, 2021). As Adam Grant explains in his book *Think Again*, "That gives us enough doubt to reexamine our old knowledge and enough confidence to pursue new insights." For children, this can be as simple as looking at the pond one morning, seeing ice on top, and saying, "Wait! That's not supposed to be like that." For teachers, it might look like reading a book that includes new research on children's development and deciding to start the day outside in free play rather than starting inside with a reading lesson. This confident humility and being open to other possibilities are rooted in and lead to curiosity—the idea that maybe we don't know all there is to know.

Confident humility aligns with the well-known concept in education of a growth mindset, or the idea that we can always learn and improve (Dweck & Leggett, 1988). Ideally, in early childhood education we are supporting the development of this confident humility and a growth mindset to set the stage for children's desire for lifelong learning.

Curiosity

Curiosity, or the desire to know about ourselves, others, and the world around us, is core to learning. Inherit in the desire to know about the world is the idea that we don't already know everything there is to know—we don't know it all. Another way to think about curiosity is looking for new experiences and embracing the novelty and unpredictability of everyday life (Kashdan et al., 2009). As Brené Brown (2021) suggests, engaging in curiosity is a vulnerable act because "it requires us to surrender to uncertainty" (p. 65). This vulnerability is true whether we're learning about our own internal world, other people, or the natural world.

Curiosity is different from "interest." Interest is being open, cognitively, to engaging with a topic or experience (Brown, 2021). Curiosity, however, requires us to know a bit about something in order to then be curious about it. Why? Because curiosity is "recognizing a gap in our knowledge about something that interests us, and becoming emotionally and cognitively invested in closing that gap through exploration and learning. Curiosity often starts with interest and can range from mild curiosity to passionate investigation" (Brown, 2021, p. 64).

As an example, imagine you are mingling at a party with someone you've just met. You likely started out interested—open to learning about them. But curiosity might not emerge until they share that they used to teach high school but decided to make the switch to teaching early childhood. You know a bit about teaching. You know the many differences (and similarities) that exist between teenagers and toddlers, so now you're suddenly curious about why they decided to make the shift in teaching.

Specific to young children, imagine a group encounters a deer while out exploring beyond the fence. One of the children says, "It's a buck! Look at its antlers!" Then another child notices the buck only has antlers on one side of his head, "Wait! Why does it only have antlers on one side? What happened?!" Both children have an understanding of what a deer is, specifically a male deer. The second child then makes an observation that runs counter to their knowledge of bucks and thus is *curious* about what happened or why the observation doesn't fit with their previous understanding.

Often, confusion or surprise will spark the shift from interest to curiosity. Surprise is "the sense of astonishment and wonder that one feels toward the unexpected" and acts as a bridge between cognition and emotion (Mellers et al., 2013). In other words, the emotion of surprise sparks the desire to explore and learn more. Both of the examples we mentioned earlier involved surprise. In the first, it was surprising that someone would shift from teaching high schoolers to teaching toddlers. In the second, it was surprising that a buck deer only had antlers on one side of its head. Not only did both examples involve surprise, or a bit of confusion, but they were also connected to previous knowledge and experiences. With a wide range of experiences, young children can more easily become emotionally and cognitively invested in exploring and learning about what confuses or surprises them. Adults play a vital role in creating a learning environment that includes a variety of experiences that support and nurture children's curiosity.

Care

The third social-emotional construct we see as vital to our work in early childhood education is that of "care." *Merriam-Webster* describes *care* as suffering of the mind, a cause of anxiety, or something that is an object of attention or anxiety. While that definition is a bit darker and worrisome—quite literally—it does encompass the idea of looking outside ourselves to other people, places, or things. Similar to curiosity, care can be both internally and externally focused. That is, children can care for themselves as well as for the world outside themselves.

At its simplest form, care is taking action to protect something, for example, a child moving a worm off the sidewalk so it doesn't get squished by a bicycle. However, there are many emotions involved in a person taking action. Two that are particularly critical are compassion and empathy. Brené Brown (2021) summarized these two emotions: "Compassion is a daily practice and empathy is a skill set that is one of the most powerful tools of compassion" (p. 118). In other words, compassion is the act, or practice, of moving the worm off the sidewalk. This is showing care, whereas empathy is a skill that allows children to understand and reflect on what someone or something is experiencing (Brown, 2021). Empathy is what leads to a child saying, "Oh, someone might step on the worm!" and leads to the action of compassion and care.

Typically, when we think of care, our first thought is caring for others or the world around us. It's important, however, for children to also learn to care for themselves. In order to do so, they must have self-awareness of their own needs and behaviors. Children can care for themselves in the way they nurture their mental and physical health. Children can also show care for themselves by setting boundaries in their interactions with others.

Like with confidence and curiosity, adults play a role in developing young children's care for other people, the natural world, and themselves. As we discuss the roles of adults in nature-based pedagogy, we will relate those roles to many areas of child development but particularly to the 3Cs.

What is nature pedagogy?

In order to frame this book, we need to define at the start our understanding of the difference and relationship between nature-based education and nature pedagogy. Nature-based education is used to describe a variety of program models that teach about the natural world. Yet these programs may or may not engage in nature pedagogy—an approach or method of teaching. Nature pedagogy is a way of working with children that acknowledges our relationship with the natural world (Warden, 2022). In other words, it embodies the idea that we are part of the natural world rather than separate from it. This is lived in all aspects of the early childhood classroom:

> Nature pedagogy is a natural way of working with children that is all encompassing, from the educational environments we create, the process of assessment and planning, through to the learning journeys that we encourage children and families to take throughout childhood.
>
> (Warden 2015, p. 14)

More specifically, nature pedagogy is defined as the art of being with nature, Inside, Outside, and Beyond (Larimore, 2019; Warden 2015). It is a way of working that places the rights of the natural world alongside the rights of humans. It is an inquiry-based, child-centered way of teaching that creates links and connections in learning for children across physical locations inside buildings, outside in outdoor areas, and into spaces beyond the gate. Simply put, nature pedagogy connects experiences across the Inside, Outside, and Beyond. However, Inside, Outside, and Beyond are much more than simply places to learn; they are also a metaphor for the learning itself.

We have both been thinking and talking about this metaphor extensively. Yes, we both see the "Inside, Outside, and Beyond" as not only physical spaces but also as a relational way of being in those spaces. We see the Inside as our individual, internal world; the Outside as our relationships with people and the planet; and the Beyond as our relationships with the global community as well as the unobservable aspects of life. These relationships differ slightly when we consider the learner (e.g., child) and the teacher (e.g., adult). Let us explain further.

Inside: Our individual and internal world

In nature-based pedagogy, "Inside" not only represents the physical indoor space but also individual, internal worlds. Often, these worlds are hidden and not frequently discussed, and we make assumptions that others have similar perspectives. After all, it's human nature to act as though we are the starring role in our own play. The reality is we are all unique. We have unique biology in the ways we're physically built, we have unique histories in terms of our experiences in the world, and we all have unique ways of thinking and behaving as a result.

Thinking about the children, this internal world ("Inside") includes their individual physical health and development (strength, balance, coordination, etc.) as well as their social-emotional and cognitive development. For example, the joy children experience, their individual identity, self-esteem, and a sense of belonging are all social-emotional aspects "Inside" of them—their internal world unique to them. The cognitive aspects of this internal world include their interests and curiosities, the skills they possess, prior experiences they've had, and so on.

These components are all true of the teacher's internal world as well. All the individual skills, knowledge, and beliefs contribute to the way a teacher interacts in the classroom. We believe self-awareness of this internal world is vital to the role of being a nature-based educator. By understanding our own internal world, we can better relate to others (which we'll discuss more in a moment). A few questions that have helped us in our thinking to explore our internal world include the following:

◆ **What is my *why* for nature-based early childhood education?** In other words, what is it about this work that gets me out of bed in the morning? If I were describing to a new friend why I do the job I do, what would I say?

- ◆ **What brings me joy?** This question isn't necessarily specific to teaching. We like to start with the first thing that comes to mind. Then we explore different aspects of life—when do I experience joy at home? At work? When I am alone or with others?

- ◆ **What frustrates me?** We all have moments where we get frustrated or annoyed. This question is designed to help us reflect on the triggers that might lead to that discomfort. Are there things about myself that frustrate me? What patterns I have repeated time and again that I wish I wouldn't? What do other people say or do that frustrates me?

- ◆ **What makes me "me"?** In answering this question, we consider all aspects of our internal world—physical, social-emotional, and cognitive. What is the story that I tell myself about who I am—how am I unique, which communities I belong to, and so on.

- ◆ **What kind of teacher am I?** The answers to the questions above are just a few of the ways that you are unique and different from your co-workers. We are all individual, unique teachers different from others. Yes, there may be similarities, but who we are individually informs how we teach and interact with young children, their families, and our co-workers. We encourage you to spend some time thinking about these interactions, how you prepare for them in advance, how you reflect and respond to interactions, and so forth.

- ◆ **What is my truth?** We all have our own lived experiences that influence who we are and what we believe. Our truth isn't the same as someone else's. In order to make a team, we need to listen to other ideas and perspectives without giving up our own truth. What is my truth?

Outside: Our relationships with people and the planet

Children have an intuitive connection to the other-than-human aspects of the natural world that can be observed when adults step back and notice. Children can engage in caring communication with a slug as equals; they can love a stone and be a bird.

The adults around them often look on as they have detached and rationalized their relationship with nature. When children engage, they do so in many ways. They have a sense of kinship with the natural world where they learn in, with, about, and for the natural world. Through this sense of compassion and empathy, they make sense of the world around them. They do this through an innate curiosity and approach to discovery that is sprinkled with problem-solving. The cycle of problem-solving develops confidence as they test and fail in their ideas and theories.

Our role as adults is to be intentional in how we support these relationships between people and the planet. In this space, self-reflection is key to the development of pedagogy. We consider our own lived experiences in the world with questions, such as the following:

- **How do I connect with children and families?** We all have our own cultural capital gathered from our family and experience. This affects how curious, confident, and caring we are about the natural world. It is important to consider how we encourage all families to connect with us.
- **How do I relate with my team about our commitment to the planet?** We can talk about how important it is that we connect to and care about the natural world, but do we live those values? How do I demonstrate care through the choices you make about power use, recycling, and so on?
- **What in the world intrigues me?** Being curious as an adult models the behavior for children. For us as authors, we connect through a sense of wonderment and enduring care about the natural world. This goes beyond our day-to-day experiences in early childhood and explores us as people.
- **What is my relationship with nature?** Taking time for ourselves to be in nature gives us the energy and capacity to be with others and the planet. Considering the question allows us, as adults, to be aware of our own and others' needs.

Beyond: Global community and the unobservable

In terms of physical location, the Beyond is the space beyond the limits of a fenced play area and into spaces where children and teachers are visitors to a space. This is typically more natural, wild spaces but can even occur in urban areas. Metaphorically, the Beyond space is indicative of a sense of freedom, a sense of wildness as a mental freedom from the overly structured experiences and environments that adults create (Warden, 2012a).

The Beyond is where adults and children alike connect to something bigger than themselves (Bailie et al., 2023; Larimore, 2011; Warden, 2012a). This includes moments of wonder, but as Dacher Keltner in his book *Awe* (2023), "[w]onder, the mental state of openness, questioning, curiosity, and embracing mystery, arises out of experiences of awe" (p. 38). So what is "awe"? Keltner explains: "Awe is the feeling of being in the presence of something vast that transcends your current understanding of the world" (p. 7). For us, we think of awe as something Beyond ourselves.

Moments of awe and experiences Beyond are often found in nature and thus are core to nature-based pedagogy. Beyond moments can also be found in human beauty such as music, visual art, kindness and compassion among strangers, and moments of deep connection as a group. Keltner (2023) groups moments of awe into the eight wonders of life: moral beauty, collective effervescence, nature, music, visual design, spirituality and religion, life and death, and epiphany.

The concept of awe can sometimes be hard to tap into. As with the Inside and Outside, we have found it helpful to pause and reflect on our connections to the Beyond. We find the following questions to be helpful:

- ◆ **When do I experience awe and wonder?** Consider the eight different wonders of life Keltner suggests. When am I in awe of others' kindness and generosity? Have I experienced awe at a concert sharing a live music experience with a large group of people? Do I have moments of awe when I see a beautiful sunset, a painting, or a building? Do I have moments of amazement at children's growth and development?

◆ **When those moments of awe and wonder occur, how do I respond?** Awe and wonder can be overwhelming feelings because they're inherently difficult to describe. Do I get goosebumps, chills, cry, or have some other feeling in my body? Do I take time to *feel* the feeling in my body before rushing to explain or describe it?

We agree with Piff et al. (2015), who suggest that "[a]we shifts people away from being the center of their own individual worlds, toward a focus on the broader social context and their place within it" (p. 897). Another way to consider this focus on the broader social context, or the Beyond as we call it, is the profession of early childhood education. We often ask ourselves the following question:

◆ **How am I influencing the field of early childhood education?** In the greater sense of our advocacy, we have a vital role to play in nature-based education and the skills of nature pedagogy. After all, nature-based pedagogy is far from mainstream. The movement is growing, but we have more work to do before all young children have experiences learning with nature as part of their day-to-day formal education.

Theory of social constructivism—The role of interactions in children's learning

Often in early childhood education, you'll hear mention of this theorist or that theory. However, it seems rare for us to take the time to really explore what that theory was arguing for and how it influences day-to-day teaching practice. Before we discuss the various roles educators play when engaging with children, it seems appropriate to be explicit about our theoretical perspectives on the role of adults in children's learning.

We describe ourselves as social constructivists or co-constructivists. (For us these terms are synonymous, it's just a matter of preference). This means we believe we develop and learn within a social world and our knowledge is primarily constructed through interactions with others. Direct interactions can be verbal or nonverbal. Verbal interactions include both statements and questions. Nonverbal interactions include gaze, position of one's body, posture, and the like. We can also interact through indirect interactions, such as reading a book someone else has written.

Whether an interaction is direct or indirect, some idea or concept is being conveyed. The learner then assimilates, or connects, this information to their previous experiences and knowledge. The interaction will either align with their previous understanding or not, which means it will either reinforce or challenge their current understanding.

As you read about each of the educator roles, you will likely notice our social-constructivist perspectives. In particular, you'll notice that each of the roles we explore are rooted in relationships and recognition that we as adults influence what and how children learn.

Organization of this book

The purpose of this book is to articulate the many roles early educators play when interacting with young children. While there are many different roles, we've focused on 11 roles we think are particularly important and strongly influence children's development. The 11 roles include the following:

Provider of space—providing children with a rich physical environment for learning Inside, Outside, and Beyond

Provider of time—to provide children with and defend their time

Provider of materials—to provide appropriate materials and resources within learning spaces

Facilitator of experiences—to plan for and facilitate children's learning

Holder of memories—to document children's learning in the moment and over time

Relationship builder—to help children build relationships with themselves, other people, and the natural world

Conversationalist—to engage with children to elicit ideas and thinking and build on each other's thoughts

Manager and modeler of risk-taking—to help children navigate taking risk

Provocateur—to create new or scaffolded learning opportunities

Mentor, guide, and leader—to consider the level of direction and structure in our role

Advocate—to advocate for children, the natural world, and children's right to be in it

While recognizably imperfect, we've generally organized the roles from foundational to complex. However, this order shouldn't be taken as a perspective on the order of importance. All of these roles are important in the early childhood classroom. Each has its own impacts and potential trade-offs, but each of these different adult roles helps create a rich, holistic learning environment for young children.

Each chapter focuses on exploring a different adult role. The chapter includes an overview of the concept, why it is important to young children's learning, and how we can bring awareness to our implementation of the adult role. At the end of each chapter, we've provided examples of language you might hear in the classroom as evidence of the adult role. We have also provided self-reflection questions to help you explore how the ideas discussed in the book play out in your practice. The final chapter of the book invites you to explore your own thoughts, feelings, and behaviors to dig even deeper into your teaching practice.

A note about language

Language can be a tricky thing. Every culture and community gives different meanings to different words. We often tease each other about our different uses of language. Claire is from Scotland and Rachel is from the United States, so there are many differences. For example, *wellies* versus *rain boots*. Our teasing is always with the utmost respect. It's a way to acknowledge the uniqueness we each bring to our work. However, we realize that the tone and intent of the written word can sometimes be difficult to interpret. This is why we want to be very clear from the beginning that our intent with the terms throughout this book is respect and inclusivity.

We use *adult*, *teacher*, and *educator* interchangeably throughout the book. In our minds, there is no distinction between these terms regarding education levels, experience, or setting. Similarly, we use the terms *program*, *school*, *center*, *setting*, and *provision* interchangeably. Our use of language is in no way expressing a priority between setting types, such as home providers and centers. We believe nature-based pedagogy can be practiced anywhere children are being cared for.

Another term that we hope you'll hear from an inclusive lens is *classroom*. It is common for the term *classroom* to refer only to the indoor learning space. However, we are nature pedagogues and believe the outdoor learning spaces are also a classroom. In other words, for us *classroom* can mean the Inside, Outside, or Beyond—they are all classroom spaces.

Self-reflection

- ◆ How do you see the role of confidence, curiosity, and care in children's development?
- ◆ How are you currently integrating the 3Cs into your teaching practice?
- ◆ What do you see as the role of interactions in children's learning? What role should teachers play in those interactions?

2

Provider of space

The space or environment we work in is different within areas of a setting, between settings in the same location, and across the climatic regions of the planet. The style of care and education is intertwined with culture and land. At a foundational level, humans used local resources to design shelters and spaces that addressed the challenges they faced which were influenced by the climate. Nature-immersive models of care and education continue to feel this connection in all aspects of their pedagogy and practice as they need to be flexible to respond to change both through daily weather changes and across the changes in the year. As education and care started to be viewed as an indoor experience, so, too, did the walls and architecture of the space become part of shaping children's experiences. There are many issues around the use of space, especially indoors, when connected to containment and behavior.

Nature pedagogy (Warden, 2022; Bailie et al., 2023) suggests that spaces are located inside; outside, which includes landscaped spaces usually attached to the building and enclosed by a boundary; and beyond the gate of that boundary into the wilder, more unpredictable spaces where space and use are defined collaboratively between children and adults. One of the key differences is the sunlight. Being outdoors increases the level of vitamin D in your body, so when we create spaces outside to settle, we contribute to the building of essential building blocks of the body.

DOI: 10.4324/9781003374053-2

Vitamin D is very important to absorb calcium so that your body can build and keep the bones strong. Furthermore, vitamin D helps you keep the level of adrenalin, serotonin, and dopamine in control, which helps you avoid sadness and more emotional fluctuations. In northern countries such as Scotland, vitamin D is recommended for all people due to reduced daylight hours in the winter months.

The design of outdoor environments has evolved from spaces that have defined set zones that replicate the indoor environment to designs that embrace the relationship and more *integrated* landscape as we see in wilder landscapes. The purpose of this book is not to design spaces but to explore our role in it. In Table 2.1, we provide some examples of the relationship of space that can emerge when you consider three locations for learning Inside, Outside, and visiting in the Beyond, each of which provides a point of difference; indeed, why repeat a space when it could easily be extended and offer something curiously different for the children?

TABLE 2.1 Examples of relationship across the Inside, Outside, and Beyond spaces

Inside	*Outside*	*Beyond*
Cooking area in home corner	Mud kitchen/laboratory	Muddy puddle, discovered spaces for making mixtures
Book corner	Laminated books/charts Story circle	Storytelling in a clearing, on a log, as you walk
Art Area/workshop area	Transient art area, painting with mud. paint onto outdoor easel	Areas scraped aside to make a space to work Found surfaces such as tree trunks, flat stones Limited selection of art materials in backpack
Woodwork bench-flat wood, organized tool access	Outdoor construction space with found wood	Tool roll in adult backpack Adult/child focus
Math area	Math focuses in the context of the mud kitchen Additional resources added in, such as measuring spoons, etc.	Math on the go— resources are found and extended by a few specific math tool like a tape measure in backpack.

By considering why you have spaces and how they are used, we can begin to explore the relationship between rather than the repetition of areas across locations.

There are many models of nature-based experiences around the world, with a variety of operational differences influenced by culture, climate, community, and curriculum; however, they are connected underneath by a meshwork of the values of nature pedagogy (Warden and Fargher, 2023). The spaces we visit regularly are referred to in Scotland as satellite sites to a main program or building, but there are also models in which the whole program is immersed in the *wilder* landscape, which is referred to as immersive. Moving beyond the gate the landscape is often actually rather managed even though we perceive it as being wilder.

This chapter examines the space and the relationship so that we can begin to consider the use of space as a social construction. This use of space supports curiosity, care, and confidence when it is considerate and intentional. Consider the impact of a wide-open field versus a cozy glade in a forest or a pathway that is straight versus a meandering one full of resting spaces. The space has an impact on our behavior and will subtly affect the experiences we take part in; the same is true for the children we work with.

Space to be in large groups

Humans are, essentially, herd animals and as such seek to gather together. In his work on the psychology of groups, Forsyth (2024) suggests that being in a large group satisfies our need to belong and allows us to achieve things that we could not on our own. It allows children to see themselves being somewhere that is popular and commonplace. Consider the following:

- ◆ Open spaces to move
- ◆ Platforms
- ◆ Slopes and amphitheaters to set large numbers of children

Space to be with one or two peers

To increase dialogue, sometimes small cozy spaces support children to engage. Not everyone has the confidence to speak out in a large group, and often using small groups allows greater depth of conversation. Supervision and engagement need to be balanced when children move into more secluded places. In a team, arranging who will be the monitor/supervisor, counting heads, and ensuring overall calm allow another staff member to relax enough to focus on the group. Consider the following:

◆ Space enclosed by a group of low bushes
◆ A log circle
◆ A tree stump as a focus space

Space to be alone

In the busy world of childhood, children appear to need time to develop the confidence to be alone. Silence, daydreaming, and being alone should move from being viewed as a lack of something to the development of confidence in being alone and within yourself. Consider the following:

◆ Space at the base of a tree, on a boulder seat
◆ An area where you can see each other but is beyond easy reach
◆ Walking/being apart from the main group

Shelter from the elements

Nature-based programs are not about survival training! In our advocacy chapter, we discuss the need to mainstream nature pedagogy rather than it being an alternative provision. Humans need shelter from the elements when they reach a point where they are unable to self-regulate. What that shelter looks like is place-specific, from a tarp hung in a tree to open-front log shelters, from yurts to Nordic huts. The principle is the same: if you are in an immersive model, you need to keep your warm outer clothes on but warm up or dry off a little so that you feel OK. As soon as the shelter becomes too indoor, it will alter the model of being indoor and outdoor. There is no problem with that; we just need to be aware that it takes time to transition. Consider the following:

- ◆ Time—How long do you want to be in the shelter?
- ◆ Year-round use—Could you shelters that you use in different seasons (e.g., snake season, snowfall)
- ◆ Purpose—warmth, access to resources, eating, rest

Movable spaces

Population growth has required us to reflect on our use of space. The impact on wilder free-ranging spaces is evident as the built environment continues to expand. And many nature-based educators and administrators seek to reconcile human impact with the rights of the natural world in their use of the spaces they access. The creation of community spaces that are temporary and therefore movable allows the impact of compaction and denudation to be managed in a balanced way. Urban Bloom is an experiment in urban space design that focuses on the need and intention rather than permanent infrastructure. https://www.archdaily.com/946464/living-in-community-13-projects-that-promote-shared-spaces

There are threads here that adults can consider that closely align with child-created spaces that support community building. Consider the following:

- ◆ Using loose parts such as movable tree stumps or thermal sitting mats to respond to the needs of children at the point of creation
- ◆ Robust permanent shelters with flexible use
- ◆ Rota for their use to minimize impact

Circular spaces

The idea of equivalence and balance has long been represented through circular shapes. From our lived experiences, children respond to a gathering circle as a settling and grounding experience. Circles are about equality and respect; they symbolize for us the idea that everyone is respected, heard, and cared for. The adult use of circles is intentional to have meetings, consult children, share stories, and draw attention to the range of ideas that children have in order to inspire others.

Creating spaces to meet and eat is an important part of any design. In outdoor nature-based spaces, they feel even more valuable which may link back to some form of genetic memory. Fire circles are an interesting facet of community building as they offer a social nexus and support prosocial behaviors. Dr Christopher Lynn, an anthropologist from the University of Alabama discovered that when 226 people watched a video of a flame flickering with sound effects, it consistently lowered blood pressure and appeared to make people more sociable. Research on alpha brainwave patterns showed that watching the movement of a flame improves levels of human comfort and satisfaction (Tamokoshi et al., 2011). It follows then that something as simple as sitting in a group circle watching a flame (Inside, Outside, or Beyond) can center children and help them self-regulate their brains. Being centered not only enables all the domains to develop more readily but also supports the development of emotive registers, such as consideration and care.

WHAT IT SOUNDS LIKE: EXAMPLES OF LANGUAGE RELATED TO USING SPACE

Space can be viewed as just the arrangement of resources or, in this case, a tool to support curiosity, care, and confidence through socially constructed experiences.

Internal language or language with co-teachers

"How could we improve the areas where children can be alone?"

"I have noticed that three or four children are seeking out a space for a specific car play they have developed."

"I wonder what would change in their play if we increased the size or the construction area?"

Language to use with children

"Where could we use to gather our treasures that we find?"

"Go as far as you can see me and I can see you."

"Here is a box of some materials like grass, sticks, and rocks that we could put outside. Can you show me using these pictures of our outside area where you think they should go?"

"Where do you like to go to be alone?"

Self-reflection

- ◆ Look at your inside and outside areas as spaces that work together.
  - ◆ How do they work together?
  - ◆ Do you repeat or extend the use of space when outside?
  - ◆ Is the outside area full of irresistible invitations? If not, why not?
- ◆ Make a map of the outside area (or your site) and note the behaviors you see, not the resources.
- ◆ Do the behaviors match the resources adults have put there? Perhaps the space gives a message to children about what to do there for you to observe.
- ◆ How does the use of space support curiosity, care, and confidence?

3

Provider of time

As the philosopher Lao Tzu said, "Time is a created thing. To say, 'I don't have time' is like saying, 'I don't want to.'" This is true in our personal lives as well as in the early childhood classroom. For example, we often hear from educators statements like, "We don't have time in our schedule to add that activity." The reality is time is all we really have in life that is truly ours. Furthermore, time is fleeting. Once it's gone, it's gone, and we can't get it back. Knowing how precious time is, the questions are, How are we choosing to use our time? Are we using classroom time in a way that supports children's learning—particularly related to confidence, curiosity, and care?

Providing time for different purposes

If we are purposeful, we can use our time in ways to support the development of curiosity, confidence, and care among young children. And it's the adults who are generally the decision-makers when it comes to using time. Thus, one of the critical roles of an early childhood educator is as a provider of time.

In order to provide time, we as educators have to let go of tight control over the schedule. This means being flexible in order to make choices based on our goals for children rather

DOI: 10.4324/9781003374053-3

than a predetermined schedule. Our goal, of course, is for children to have meaningful experiences and deeper learning. The fact is that deep learning takes time and requires a slower pace. Another component of embracing a slower pace is spending time on the important things rather than drivel. For example, it's common in early childhood to observe a class waiting for one particular child to sit down crisscross applesauce, whereas what really matters during large-group instruction is conversation and connection with each other—not how one child has positioned their body.

The fact is that both nature and children slow down and take time. Very little in nature happens quickly. Instead, nature changes slowly over days, weeks, months, and even years. Similarly, children naturally take time to explore, play, grow, and develop. So our role as adults is to embrace both nature and child time and provide children with as much time as possible in their time. This time is provided for a variety of different purposes including to play, experience a full range of emotions, and to just be—including in nature. In the following, we explore these different purposes of providing time. Table 3.1 provides a summary of how these different purposes support the development of children's curiosity, care, and confidence.

Time for play

Play in its truest form involves an active, alert, but non-stressed frame of mind (Gray, 2013). As Dr. Peter Gray (2013) explained, "Attention is attuned to the activity itself, and there is reduced consciousness of self and time." Being unaware of time is the opposite of the pressure a child feels in the morning getting ready for school. You know the pressure: "Hurry up! Get your backpack! We're late." In the early childhood classroom, we want children to experience play as much as possible. Specific to time, our goal is for them to be unaware of time as much as possible.

To do this, we can provide large chunks of time throughout the day for play. There are many different definitions of play, but Dr. Peter Gray (2008, 2013) summarized them into five key characteristics:

1. Play is self-chosen and self-directed.
2. Play is activity in which the means are more valued than the ends.
3. Play has structure, or rules, that are not dictated by physical necessity but emanate from the minds of the players.
4. Play is imaginative, nonliteral, and mentally removed in some way from "real" or "serious" life.
5. Play involves an active, alert, but non-stressed frame of mind.

Thus, when we provide uninterrupted time for play, we are providing time during which children choose which activities they want to engage with, when children are establishing the rules, and during which they are relaxed. This means 60 minutes or more at a time during which there is no teacher-led activity, such as a large-group activity, a small-group activity, snack time, transitioning to another location, and so on. These large swaths of time allow children to get into what Mihalyi Csikszentmihalyi (1990) called "flow." This flow is where time seems to whiz by because they are so immersed in what they are doing.

This play can take on many different forms or types of play. In his book *Evolutionary Playwork*, Bob Hughes (2011) described 16 different types of play to consider when providing time for children's play, such as imaginative play, rough-and-tumble play, and exploratory play. By providing time, we give children the opportunity to explore many different types of play in deep, meaningful ways. Of course, the environment for that play—such as space, materials, and interactions with others—is important as well. Those adult roles for supporting play are explored in other chapters of this book.

Time to notice
Another important purpose of providing time is for children to notice. Slowing down gives children time to observe both the human and natural worlds around them. Imagine slowing down at snack time so a child might notice their own reflection in their spoon as they eat their applesauce. This, in turn, provides opportunities for the adult to extend the conversation with a question

like "Does your reflection look the same on both sides of the spoon?" Outside, slowing down might give a child enough time to notice a row of ants moving from one place to another or hear a pair of birds calling back and forth to each other.

Not only do children need time to notice in the moment, but they also need time to notice patterns over time. For example, a child might stop and notice the same tree every day. After a few months, they might notice a few leaves at the top starting to change colors. By allowing time to notice the observations of the tree have become personal and integrated into the child's life, bringing more meaning to the leaf-changing phenomenon than if an adult had simply pointed out the tree and leaves. In other words, the child has ownership of the noticing because they were given time.

Time to fail and try again

A vital part of learning is failure or making mistakes. As John Dewey (1988) said, "Failure is instructive. The person who really thinks learns quite as much from his failures as from his successes." Young children need time to try something, fail, evaluate, and try again. These failures might look like attempts at building a tower out of blocks, writing their name, or climbing up onto a stump. Similarly, children need time to create something (e.g., a drawing, a game, a story) and then time to revise and innovate. These revisions are often based on a failure of some sort—meaning they didn't achieve the desired outcomes or qualities of what they were creating. For example, a drawing might not look like the child had intended. Or the rules of the game they created might allow too many points to be earned. These kinds of revisions are plentiful in children's play.

Whatever the task, children need the time for multiple attempts. And once they've solved the problem or completed the task, they also need time to perfect that task through repetition. In other words, as adults, we have to provide enough time for children to attempt a task, learn from their failures, and then try again in order to turn the failure into a success. This requires patience and once again slowing down to embrace children's pace.

Time to experience and sit with emotion

Often learning is thought of as a cognitive process, but let us not forget that every type of learning—whether cognitive or physical—also includes social-emotional learning. The fact is that all humans are emotional beings before thinking beings and that emotions strongly influence our thinking (Mlodinow, 2022). This means that we have physical reactions in our body before we ever make a cognitive connection or analysis. (By the way, this is true of both children and adults, which is important to remember when we're interacting with children.) As we mature, we're better able to regulate these emotions. This is emotional intelligence, that is, the ability to recognize and express emotion, connect the emotion to thought, and then self-regulate those emotions (Mayer, Salovey, & Caruso, 2000).

Children experience many emotions as they're moving through and learning about the world. For example, failure, as mentioned earlier, may be accompanied by frustration, envy, overwhelm, or any number of other feelings. While learning, children may also experience sadness when they leave their family for the day. Or they may experience frustration or anger with their peers and need time to process those feelings before resolving the conflict. One of our foundational roles as adults is to provide children with enough time to experience, sit with, acknowledge, and move through those emotions in order to develop children's emotional intelligence.

Time to build relationships

Many of the emotions children experience are a result of inter-acting with other people. In a later chapter, we discuss in detail the important role adults play in helping children build rela-tionships with themselves, others, and the broader world. Here, however, we want to draw attention to the fact that developing these relationships requires time. When building relationships with others, children need time for conversations and shared experiences and to reflect individually and together on those experiences. Again, we discuss in subsequent chapters many of these relationship-building topics, but it's important to note here the role of time for these relationships to develop.

Time to just be

We live in a frenetic world that seems to constantly be demanding something from us, including the notifications on our phones saying, "Pay attention to me!" While young children don't have cell phones, they do feel the energy of the world around them— the constantly moving, fast-paced, must-do, or be-something energy. We can give children refuge from that world by providing them with time to just be—to enjoy "nothing" time. Do you remember sitting in the grass mindlessly scraping at the dirt with a stick? Or lying on the grass and watching the clouds float by overhead? These are moments of simply being in the world—no agenda, no deep cognitive, emotional, or physical activity. This time to "just be" is so important for young children.

In addition to the power of calm, time to just be will eventually run its course. That is, if given enough time children will become bored. Boredom means that they're ready to do something else (Bench & Lench, 2013). You may be wondering why in the world we as teachers would want children to be bored! Well, boredom makes it more likely that children will have experiences related to social, emotional, cognitive, and physical development that could have been missed otherwise (Bench & Lench, 2013). In other words, boredom can stimulate meaningful learning (Kets de Vries, 2014). This results after they've had plenty of time to "just be." During this time, children's imaginative worlds can open, allowing them to create and dream. In other words, during this time, they can connect with their inner world, the world outside of them, and the greater world beyond.

Time to be in and learn with the natural world

Children have a right to be in and with the natural world. Yet, as you're likely aware, children are spending less and less time outdoors and more and more time in front of screens. In 2010, a Kaiser Family Foundation study found that 8- to 18-year-old children averaged 7.5 hours of screen time each day (Rideout, Foehr, & Roberts, 2010). During the COVID-19 pandemic, children's screen time increased by two hours (Hedderson, et al., 2023). A review of the psychological impacts of both screen time and green time suggests that time outdoors in nature may buffer the negative consequences of screen time (Oswald et al., 2020). The authors even go so far as to suggest nature may be an "underutilized public health resource" for children's psychological well-being (Oswald et al., 2020, p. 39). Thus, another role of teachers is to provide the children with time to be in and learn from the natural world. "When children spend all day, every day, in a fully immersive space, they develop a sense of the variety and complexity of the natural world" (Warden, 2022, p. 27).

One reason this time with the natural world matters is that research has shown that frequent positive outdoor experiences in childhood, along with an adult who modeled interest in the natural world, lead to pro-environmental behaviors later in life (Chawla & Hart, 1995; D'Amore & Chawla, 2018). By the way, now seems a good time to mention that more recent research suggests that significant life experiences in the outdoors are a factor in early childhood educators integrating nature-based approaches into their teaching (Schaefer, 2022). So, more nature now may mean more nature-based teaching in the future.

Time for silence

The world is an incredible place—both the natural and human worlds. Most of the time, the world is also a very loud and hectic place. Sometimes we need time for silence in order to observe and/or feel the world around us. We need silence to hear our own thoughts. We need silence to feel our feelings. As Eckart Tolle (2004) said, "Words reduce reality to something the human mind can grasp, which isn't very much" (p. 27). When we try to put words to what we're experiencing, our words often fall short. All this is to say that sometimes we need to simply be silent and feel the emotions without trying to explain or analyze the feelings. For example, children may silently watch a group of ants crawling along a log. Or together we might pause and notice the way the sunshine sparkles on the frost in a field. As we work with children, one of our roles is to allow for these moments of silence—to resist the urge to be constantly narrating the world and instead just be silent and experience what is. This silence can bring calm, clarity, and connection. In other words, often silence is where the magic happens.

In relation to curiosity, care, and confidence, let us pull out the specific aspects of time that may support their development.

TABLE 3.1 Examples of how providing time supports the 3Cs

Time to...	In support of ...		
	Curiosity	Care	Confidence
Play	Open-ended, child-initiated, self-fulfilling	Awareness of the status we all have and how it makes us feel	Testing and exploring boundaries within a safe space
Notice	Ability to see and respond to fascinations	Seeing when you can help yourself and others; the impact you have is a skill	Noticing the small tasks achieved and challenges builds a sense of affirmation
Fail and try again	Cycles of testing and experimentation	Awareness of self-care and inner narratives	Development of a growth mindset
Build relationships	Awareness of the endless things to discover and your place as a human in that relationship	The understanding of reciprocity (give and take) in relationships	Testing social risk-taking in a space that understands
Just be	Assimilation and processing of thoughts and feelings	Self-awareness and comfort of being alone	Boredom/daydreaming as a provocation for creative thinking and inspiration
Learn in and with the natural world	Contextual, authentic, and place-based learning	Responsive to our actions—positive context for care of self and others	Clear feedback loops to our own behaviors and actions
Be silent	Develops the use of all senses to discover the world	Awareness of own thinking, adults allowing children to feel attention	Providing opportunities for thoughts and ideas to develop that the child can then share

Embracing the pace of children and nature

It is human nature to want results quickly, and yet the best things in life take time—long stretches of time. As Lao Tzu said, "Nature does not hurry, yet everything is accomplished." This is why it's so important to embrace the time and pace of nature and children. In doing so, we provide them with the time they need to play, fail, and try again, develop emotional intelligence, and be in and experience the beauty of the world through both active engagement and silent observation.

For us as adults, this means slowing down and patiently letting go of our preconceived notions of what we "should be doing right now" to focus on the children and their needs. This isn't to say we should abandon the schedule altogether. In fact, as writer Annie Dillard (1989) suggested, the way we spend our days is how we spend our lives. Thus, it's important to have a general schedule, so we "spend the days" on important things. However, when it comes to early childhood, it is vital to have a schedule that allows children time to learn and grow. We think of this as a general flow to the day, with predictable parts of the day and general order but flexibility to allow for the interests and needs of children at any given moment. The ideal schedule ignores the frenzied pace of the adult world and embraces the pace of children and nature. As Ruth Wilson (2012), a trailblazer in early childhood environmental education, wisely said:

> Natural environments offer rich opportunities for play, creativity, and reflection. Children should be given the time to benefit from these rich opportunities. Providing this time—and guarding it from intrusions—should be viewed as one of the primary responsibilities of teachers and parents.
>
> (p. 47)

In this chapter, we've highlighted the importance of providing time for children and hopefully convinced you to guard that time from intrusions. Providing time is such a foundational role that we've separated it from other roles, but it's also core to many of the other roles we explore in this book. For example, facilitating experiences and building relationships both require providing time. So as you consider the many other roles nature-based educators play in children's learning, also keep in mind the importance of time in each of those roles.

WHAT IT SOUNDS LIKE: EXAMPLES OF LANGUAGE RELATED TO PROVIDING TIME

Providing time for young children requires lots of inner thought, conversation with co-teachers, and even conversations with the children themselves. Here are a few examples.

Internal language or language with co-teachers

"Should we extend free play a few more minutes since they seem so engaged with play?"

"The group seems restless with this large-group activity. Maybe we should cut it short and allow more choice time."

"Wow, they're really enjoying just sitting here chatting with each other as they eat snacks. Let's not rush this."

Language to use with children

"Would you like to keep playing or are you ready to go on our hike?"

"It looks like you're making progress on your construction project. Would you like a few more minutes to keep building?"

"I notice people are starting to get restless sitting here as a group. Would you like to go outside and play now?"

Self-reflection

♦ This week, make note of how your class time is spent each day. How much time is spent on each portion of the day? Do these time allotments align with your planned daily schedule? Which portions of the day are getting more/ less time than originally planned?

♦ This week, also make note of how decisions to move on to the next activity are being made. Who is driving the decisions? What is driving the decisions (e.g., children's engagement with play, children saying they're hungry, time on the clock)?

4

Provider of materials

In addition to providing the valuable resource of time, adults provide another important resource in children's learning—materials. Educators provide materials in all three learning spaces (i.e., Inside, Outside, and Beyond) as opportunities for children to play and make sense of the world around them. Every item provides different affordances, or types of opportunities, for children's play. Thus, one of our roles as educators is being intentional about selecting and introducing materials to the classroom. We can intentionally select the materials themselves, how many materials are added to learning spaces, and how we as adults introduce those materials into the classroom.

Types of materials and their play opportunities

Different materials provide different affordances, or opportunities, for play. Generally, when we say "materials," we are referring to objects that are movable rather than fixed elements. Fixed elements might include built features such as a stage, cabin, or balance beam or natural features, such as a large downed tree that is immovable. While moveable materials can also be manufactured or natural, they are items children can transport from one location to another. For example, movable materials might include stumps, sticks, rocks, buckets, shovels, or ropes. For the role of "provider of materials," we are focusing on movable

DOI: 10.4324/9781003374053-4

materials. (We have included a discussion of fixed elements in Chapter 2: "Provider of Space.") Our goal is to provide materials that vary in play opportunities and have a range of complexity.

You may have noticed that we haven't referred to these movable materials as "toys," and there is a reason for that. Movable materials can have a singular purpose or be open-ended. We think of toys as objects that can generally be used for one type of play. Toys direct children's play. This means toys do not provide a variety of play opportunities. In contrast, open-ended materials can be used in an endless number of ways. In early childhood, we often refer to these open-ended materials as "loose parts."

Loose parts is a term that was originally coined by landscape architect Simon Nicholson. In 1971 he described the theory of loose parts: "In any environment, both the degree of inventiveness and creativity, and the possibility of discovery, are directly proportional to the number and kind of variables in it" (p. 30). In other words, loose parts are simply variables in children's play—they provide possibilities for play.

By providing loose parts, we reduce the amount of "stuff" we need to have in a learning space. These possibility-rich materials also inherently support all the different developmental domains. For example, a bucket might become a step stool for a child to investigate a bird's nest on a branch—physical development as well as science. The next day, it might be used to haul special "jewels" in the children's make-believe jewelry store. This storytelling play supports not only physical development with the carrying but also cooperation with others and language and literacy development in creating a storyline.

When providing materials for young children on any scale, our goal is to provide materials that have many possibilities for play and thus support all developmental domains. We have assumed there will be sensorial encounters across all of them.

If we hold these possibilities in our heads, we can consider what aspects we need to develop in their space and what they offer to children (see Table 4.1). Furthermore, they demonstrate that natural elements can be brought into any space, from a small balcony to a large outdoor area. When we use the elements and the skills, concepts, and knowledge, they can support children to discover that there is no reason why any space cannot embrace nature pedagogy.

TABLE 4.1 Examples of concepts, skills, and knowledge possible with materials

Material/ feature	Concepts	Skills	Knowledge
Rock	Strength Durability Erosion	Grinding Climbing Prospecting	Origin—sedimentary, metamorphic, igneous Dimensions Names of types
Grass	Growth Energy	Cutting Twisting Pulling	Variety Care Colors
Water	Power Movement Transformation	Damming Directing Floating	Speed Position language— around, down. passed Name of features— pond, river, rain
Sticks	Power Structures— stability / balance Attachment	Bending Cutting Carrying	Variety Strength Hard/softwood
Leaves	Decay Growth Opacity	Folding Cutting Throwing	Leaf shapes/features Area Food—photosynthesis
Flowers	Color Death and decay Beauty	Picking Arranging Tending	Seed formation Biodiversity Variety
Shells	Movement/ attachment to rocks Beauty Resilience	Collecting Patterning Threading	Materials (relationship between sand and shell) Variety and formation
Sunlight/ shadow	Time Distortion Opacity	Dancing Walking Responding	Solid/transparency Materials Movement of sun/moon

Selecting materials for the classroom

At this point, after we've gone on and on about the power of loose parts, it wouldn't be outlandish to assume selecting materials for the classroom is as simple as selecting open-ended materials. While that is a great starting point, we can be even more intentional in providing materials for young children. In addition to considering the open-endedness of materials, we can also consider whether materials are authentic, developmentally appropriate, value diversity, relate to nature in meaningful ways, and are sustainable. We'll discuss each of these in more.

Authentic materials

What does it mean for materials to be "authentic"? For us, "authentic materials" means real objects that would be used day-to-day or found in the natural world.

A good test for this is asking, "Would adults use this item?" For example, in the dramatic play area, there might be miniature toy replicas of cans of soup. An authentic alternative would be to have real cans of soup. The real cans will be heavier, wider, and have more environmental print. With one simple move of adding a real can of soup, we've provided greater opportunities for children to develop their physical strength in lifting, gripping, and so on. The children might try to stack the cans, which engages their cognitive problem-solving skills. They might then get frustrated with trying to problem solve and now are learning to regulate their emotions.

That's the power of authentic materials—they provide greater opportunities for true holistic development! Authentic materials vary in size, weight, texture, and shape, which provides more opportunities for physical, cognitive, and social-emotional development.

By using authentic materials in the classroom, we also send a message to children that we see them as capable. It sends the message that they are capable of carrying a real plate. That they are creative enough to make their own sandwich from loose parts rather than playing with a piece of plastic formed into the shape of a sandwich. Sure, children may need adult help in developing the skills to use some materials, but that is us conveying the underlying belief that we see them as capable. That we know they can do it and we're willing to invest the time, energy, and patience to help them get there.

Authenticity requires some honesty around what ideas, or values the materials represent. What is the silent message they convey? If we always share baby piglets in our farm sets because they are adorable, where do we show the sow and the boar? Children are capable of understanding complex ideas when authentic natural materials are used. As the adult, we ask ourselves, "Is this made of or depicting real nature?" In other words, do the materials show caricatures of nature or do they represent living and nonliving things that are actually found in the natural world? We'll talk more about nature-related materials later, but we would be remiss to not mention it here as well in the context of authentic materials.

Developmentally appropriate materials

A further consideration when selecting materials is whether they are developmentally appropriate. This means the materials should match the skills and abilities of the children you are with, while also providing opportunities for them to grow and build on those skills and abilities. Would you give a chainsaw to a 3-year-old? No, of course not. They don't have the strength or the skills to manage such a wieldy tool. However, it would be developmentally appropriate to support them in using a small hand saw by providing a safe space, protective tools, and rules for how to use the tool without hurting themselves or others. When considering developmentally appropriate materials, we can ask the following questions:

◆ **Is the item appealing and interesting to children?** Our goal with adding materials isn't just to have more "stuff" in the area. We don't want clutter but, rather, materials full of potential. Everything added to the classroom should have the potential to be interesting to children. This doesn't mean you have to know for sure that it will appeal to children—items can always be removed if they're not of interest and simply taking up space.

◆ **Will this material support children's learning through play? Does it contribute to the mix of play opportunities in the classroom and thus support a variety of developmental domains?** We are striving for materials that provide a wide variety of play opportunities (e.g., construction play, dramatic play, water play) and in all developmental domains (i.e., physical, social-emotional, and cognitive).

◆ **Will this material encourage cooperation and playing with others?** Independent play is not only valuable, but we also want to support young children in building their skills to positively interact with other children. Materials that encourage cooperative play can better help us achieve this goal.

◆ **Is the material safe for use by children independently? Could it be safely used with adult supervision?** Materials that require adult supervision have a place in the classroom (see Chapter 9: "Manager and Modeler of Risk-Taking"). However, we also want to provide materials that children can safely use on their own. By asking this question about safety we're bringing intention to the mix of independent and adult-supported play.

◆ **Is the item free of other hazards (e.g., toxic finishes, choking hazards)?** Some materials have the potential for harm and both adults and children have little influence on reducing the risk of harm. Materials with small parts could pose a choking hazard for our youngest children and so would not be appropriate in the classroom. The material the objects are made with can also be problematic. This might include being made with lead or other toxic materials.

Materials that value diversity

Just as natural ecosystems are healthier when they're diverse, our human systems are stronger when they include a diversity of people. Furthermore, nature-based pedagogy is built on the belief that all children, no matter their background or ability, have a right to experience positive outdoor experiences. With this in mind, classroom materials should reflect the backgrounds, knowledge, and experiences of the children and families in the program. This means reflecting, without reinforcing stereotypes, the diversity of family structures, race, ethnicity, physical abilities, and so on. This includes materials such as toys, games, loose parts, books, and dramatic play materials, such as dress-up clothes. It also includes the displays and decorations that may surround children's learning spaces—even if they don't have direct interaction with the materials.

When we think of diversity one thing that might not be as obvious, but is important related to nature-based education, is illustrating the many different ways to experience and enjoy the natural world. Outdoor experiences span a wide range from adventure-based physical activities, such as backcountry skiing, to nature study-based activities, such as birding. Just as we strive to represent and reflect the range of diversity with such things as language, food, and customs, it's important to also consider the range of outdoor activities. Some families in the classroom community might enjoy bird-watching on the weekend. The dramatic play area could include birding vests, bird books, and binoculars. Similarly, there might be a strong camping culture in your community so tents and backpacks might be another addition to the materials available for children's play. Consider outdoor activities such as hiking, camping, fishing, hunting, skiing, snowmobiling, painting, gardening, picnicking, horseback riding, geocaching, canoeing, biking, and so much more!

Not only should materials mirror children's lives, but they should also serve as a window into the world of children from different backgrounds, including those that may not be represented in the school community. In other words, materials serve as metaphorical mirrors (reflecting children's experiences) and windows (offering a view of the outside world). Materials also serve as what Sims Bishop (1990) referred to as "sliding glass doors." Sims Bishop discussed the sliding glass door concept in relation to books because readers "have only to walk through in imagination to become part of whatever world has been created or recreated by the author" (p. 1).

The mirror, window, and sliding door metaphor is not limited to books. Reflecting and valuing diversity includes all materials in the classroom spaces (i.e., Inside, Outside, or Beyond), including displays, informational texts, fictional texts, toys, games, dramatic play materials, and loose parts. By providing materials with diversity in mind, we are creating an inclusive learning environment that conveys each child is unique and their uniqueness makes for a stronger learning community—it is an asset for everyone's learning.

Nature-related materials

Nature-based pedagogy is a way of teaching that encourages children's development of a relationship with the natural world. One way this relationship is developed is by interacting with materials that are either made of or relate to nature in some way. Materials made of nature might include things such as pine cones, acorns, leaves, tree bark, and the like. Materials that relate to nature might include story books, informational texts, tools for exploring such as magnifying glasses, classroom documentation and decoration, dramatic play clothes and tools, and so much more.

Materials made of nature can be found locally. When collecting materials please be aware of the environmental impact focusing primarily on dead materials that have fallen to the ground—also known as "dead and down." Also be aware of repeatedly collecting materials from the same locations to minimize impact. Materials that relate to nature may be able to be created (discussed later), but some will need to be purchased. Whether creating or purchasing materials, we encourage you to consider the following principles when selecting nature-related materials (Larimore, 2019; Bailie, Larimore, Pikus, 2023):

1. Emphasize natural instead of manufactured when possible.
2. Choose authentic instead of cartoon-like materials.
3. Avoid stereotypes of both humans and nature.
4. Select materials that represent local nature.
5. Ensure materials reflect a diversity of people having positive outdoor experiences.
6. Choose materials that help to connect the indoors to the outdoors.
7. Select materials that encourage disciplinary development (e.g., literacy, math, science) and connections with nature.

Ultimately, when it comes to selecting nature-related materials the goal is to encourage children to learn *with* nature by selecting materials that provide varied sensory experiences, connect to outdoor experiences, and encourage a relational way of being with the natural world.

Sustainable materials

A core principle of nature-based pedagogy is recognizing humans and nature are interconnected. Practicing environmental sustainability in providing materials—whether purchasing or creating them—is one way to live that principle. In other words, an opportunity to embody the "care" we've discussed throughout this book.

Here are a few things to consider when it comes to the environmental impact of material selection:

Was the material manufactured locally? The farther something has to travel, the greater the environmental impact. When possible, choose materials that have been made of locally sourced materials.

Is the item made from a durable material? In other words, will it hold up to young children and outdoor elements such as extreme temperatures, changes in humidity, sunlight, being dragged through the dirt, and so on?

If it's a consumable item, is it refillable or rechargeable? For example, rather than purchasing single-use watercolor squirt bottles, is there paint concentrate available to refill the art supply?

Is it easy to repair the item if (when!) it breaks? Young children can be hard on materials and sometimes they break. If we can easily repair the item when it breaks, then it will reduce the need to purchase an entirely new item.

Is the item easy to repurpose or recycle when it breaks or is no longer functional? Even if an item isn't easy to repair when it breaks, there may be ways to use the item for another purpose—at least temporarily keeping it out of the landfill. If it can't be repurposed, can the material be recycled?

Creating versus purchasing materials

With those ideas in mind regarding the selection of materials, the next question is whether to purchase materials to provide for children or to create the materials. Most likely we'll purchase materials that are complicated to make or would take a long time to make. After all, time is a valuable resource in an early childhood educator's life—it must be used wisely. This is particularly true for nonconsumable materials, those that will be used more than once. For example, things like magnifying glasses, books, and furniture will most likely be purchased. Now these might be created by and purchased from a local artist, but they aren't materials the teachers and children will create together.

There may be, however, some situations in which it makes more sense to create materials rather than purchase them. For example, making play dough from scratch. In some cases, making materials can reduce the environmental impact, but beyond the environmental impacts, there are other benefits for teachers and children in creating materials. The process of creating materials can be fulfilling, joyful, and we might also learn or refine new skills. Beyond creating for ourselves, sometimes there is pleasure in creating for other people. For example, painting a rock to give to someone or weaving individualized placemats for children and teachers to use during snack time. If you're interested in making your own materials from nature, a resource to check out is *The Organic Artist for Kids: A DIY Guide to Making Your Own Eco-Friendly Art Supplies From Nature* by Nick Neddo.

Curiosity might be sparked by a thought or question like "Could I make that myself?" Then confidence might be built as the teacher or child creates something they're proud of. Finally sharing with others something that took time, energy, and thoughtfulness to create can be a beautiful expression of care for others.

In the classroom, teachers can encourage a making culture. That is, teachers can regularly prompt, "How could we make that?" or "I think we could make something like that. Should we try?" Or even more directly, lead small- and large-group activities during which children create materials. For example, the group might mix watercolors, make their own charcoal, or gather materials to weave a small basket to hold treasures in the classroom. In addition to creating a making culture within the classroom, we can create a fixing culture as well. "Oh, the stick you were using to hold up the edge of your fort broke? How could we fix it?" The teacher could then guide the children in gathering natural materials, ropes, or something similar to lash the two parts of the pole together.

All of this to say, there are benefits and challenges to both creating and purchasing materials for the nature-based classroom.

We are not so bold as to take a stance as to what percentage of materials should be made versus created. There are just too many variables to make a claim like that. What we are taking a stand on is the importance of being thoughtful and having intention when selecting materials—both the item itself and how it will be acquired.

Introducing materials to the classroom

When you've decided which materials to add to the classroom and whether they'll be made or purchased, it is time to be thoughtful about how materials will be introduced. There are a few different ways to approach this, and each approach comes with trade-offs. There really is no right or wrong way to introduce the materials. The importance is that we, as much as possible, make a conscious choice.

There are several different ways to add materials to the classroom which we can choose from at any given moment.

♦ **Before they arrive**. Before the children arrive for the day, we could add materials to the classroom for them to discover after they arrive. For example, we might put shovels out by a mud puddle.

♦ **Handing materials to children**. A more direct approach might be to hand children the materials or add them while children are present and noticing at the beginning of the session. Then, we can choose to provide an explanation for the item or not. Continuing with the shovel example, while children are playing in the puddle, we might say, "I notice you're digging with your heel to make the puddle deeper. I thought you might like this tool," and then put the shovels down without explaining how shovels work. Yet another option is to simply leave the shovels near where children are playing without saying a word.

♦ **Introducing them to children in the session**. There may be times when it is appropriate to introduce materials more formally—with or without instruction. This could be done with small groups of children or the class as a whole. This is probably most appropriate when the item is something the children haven't experienced before, may not be obvious how to use, and/or requires unique safety measures. For example, if the children have been interested in hauling things a teacher might want to introduce the idea of pulleys for hauling things up and down. The teacher could provide a minimal explanation such as "This end clips to the clothesline and then the rope goes through here," or they might guide the children through those instructions and then help the children test it out.

Each of these approaches to introducing materials has benefits and potential trade-offs. Table 4.2 highlights each approach and some of the pros and cons.

TABLE 4.2 Different approaches to introducing materials and the possible trade-offs

Approach	Examples	Pros	Cons
Adding materials to the environment when children are not present	◆ Teacher adds an aquarium with fish to the indoor classroom ◆ Teacher adds a cookbook & recipe cards to the mud kitchen ◆ Teacher puts cookie cutters in the art area	◆ Child-led—children will discover it on their own & then choose how to engage ◆ Children learn through play how to use the item	◆ Children might not discover the item
Handing material to children or putting it near children during play	◆ While children are playing in the mud kitchen, the teacher sets down a giant whisk without saying a word.	◆ Child-led—children will discover it on their own and then choose how to engage ◆ Children learn through play how to use the item	◆ Children might not discover the item ◆ Might disrupt the flow of children's play
Introducing a material in small or large groups (allowing children to explore the new item prior to any explanation by the teacher)	◆ "I brought something new you might want to try." ◆ "Isn't that fun to use? It's called a …" ◆ "Here are things you can use to create with."	◆ Draws children's attention so they know the item is present ◆ Allows for children's ideas & innovations re: how to use the item	◆ Not entirely child-led

(Continued)

TABLE 4.2 (Continued)

Approach	Examples	Pros	Cons
Teaching about **materials as a small or whole group** *(providing children with information about the item before they have a chance to explore it)*	◆ "I want to show you something new we have in the classroom. Here's how it works …" ◆ "When you use this you must …"	◆ Draws children's attention so they know the item is present ◆ Clear directions for items that are complex to use or have safety concerns	◆ Not play-based or child-led

WHAT IT SOUNDS LIKE: EXAMPLES OF LANGUAGE RELATED TO PROVIDING MATERIALS

By selecting open-ended materials, we are providing children with rich opportunities for play. However, we can be even more intentional by thinking carefully about which materials will support children's current interests. Here are some examples of language we might hear when being intentional about introducing materials:

Internal language or language with co-teachers

"Do you think we should add different materials to the dramatic play area?"

"The children seem really interested in building tall things. What could we add to the outdoor play area to help them build?"

"They're really excited about digging and pouring. I wonder how they'd play with commercial kitchen–sized spoons, ladles, and colanders."

Language to use with children

"I notice you are hauling things across the play yard. Did you know we have a wheelbarrow over there?"

"Here, I thought you might like this" (Teachers hands the child a shovel.)

"Oh, you're trying to make this tower taller? What do we have that could help you solve that problem?"

Self-reflection

♦ Take time to reflect on what materials you added or removed from the classroom this week:
   ♦ How did you decide what to add or remove?
   ♦ What impact did those changes have on children's play?
   ♦ How did you introduce the materials?
   ♦ How do you think the way the materials were introduced influenced the play?
♦ How often do you typically add or remove materials to the classroom?
♦ Do children have ready access to materials, or must they ask an adult for materials?
♦ How do you encourage children to be curious and confident enough to ask for materials?
♦ To what extent is there a *making* culture in your classroom? In what ways does this support children's confidence?
♦ To what extent is there a *fixing* culture in your classroom? How does this support the concept of care?

5

Facilitator of experiences

Planning for children's learning

There is a need for adults to be intentional in what they do Inside, Outside, and Beyond. However, there is a tension between planning too tight a program with little place-based connection and giving autonomy and agency to children so that they feel a connection to experiences. If we are to embrace nature pedagogy, then we need to consider the rhythm and flow of the natural world over the year. In most parts of the world, there are weather changes that are felt, observed, and spoken about. These drive an emergent curriculum as they are what children encounter; why would we explore snow when there isn't any outside the door? The closer the relationship between a lived experience and the play environment, the easier it is for children to bring prior knowledge to the play, or indeed to a playful inquiry.

The first step many adults take is in the area of resourcing as noted in an earlier chapter. In terms of planning, there are levels of complexity. The first is to put interesting resources into the areas for children to play with, going all the way through to planning that focuses on larger concepts like water movement and change.

Outdoor play resources can often be similar to the indoor ones but used in a different context such as a home corner/

DOI: 10.4324/9781003374053-5

mud kitchen. In areas that are designed with nature at the center the need for adult-created landscapes and materials is much lower, which, in turn, allows the child to direct where they want to go. These locations embedded in the naturescape are full of high autonomy and are referred to nominally as "the beyond the gate" (Warden 2015). They can be present inside a fence in large outdoor areas where the adults embrace nature pedagogy as the space embraces a free-ranging offering of materials that children can use in many ways.

The question is, How does an adult support learning with nature through intentional planning that embraces a more open consultative approach? Let us go through four stages of thinking about it step by step in the tables in this chapter to demonstrate an increasing complexity. We start with a basic response and move to high-quality adult planning.

Stage 1. Noticed something and made a change to resources

In Table 5.1, we can see that an adult has noticed a child's interest in an area. They note it down on the planning sheet and then put everything in the area in one go. The key here is that there should be resources in the mud kitchen all the time; what we do in planning is add detail. This detail, such as dry sand for salt or a potato masher for mud, responds to the observations we make and the theories children have. It should take weeks so that children have time to really fully experience it. One week at Auchlone Nature Kindergarten was just focused on making tea!

Let us move onto Stage 2 where the adult slows down the introduction of the resources.

TABLE 5.1 Stage 1 mud kitchen example

Observation	Children interested in mud kitchen
Response	Add more pans, mud, sticks

Stage 2. Noticed something; took action; changed resources over a number of days

Table 5.2 includes the adult's observation of what children do with the resources provided and then how they extend children's interests and engagement by changing the resources. This case study example focuses on one learning area—the mud kitchen. It demonstrates the link between resources and the adult's observations.

Consider the fact that not everything is put in the area straight away, but a core provision creates a basis. Through documenting and planning, the adult shifts and adjusts the contents to support curiosity. Through demonstrating care, the adult models how to care for the resources and the environment.

TABLE 5.2 Stage 2 mud kitchen example

Mud kitchen initial setup	◆ Variety of sizes and types of pans, cake tins, teapots, cups, bowls, sieves ◆ Tree stump seats/wooden table ◆ Access to mud
Observation summary	The children have been fascinated by the way the water moves objects around the bowl when they stir it
Resource change	◆ Lighter weight materials nearby or in containers to "go shopping" ◆ Pine needles, dry leaves ◆ Larger bowls and check access to spoons and sticks
Observation summary	The children discovered some dry dirt underneath the table area and talked about why it was dry. "Let's make it the sprinkles or salt"; "My dad uses spices at home when he cooks tea."
Resource change	◆ Provision of 3 or 4 containers with dry earth, leaves crumbled up and out of date spices available in the cooking area
Observation summary	A great engagement with the dry materials. Greater cultural engagement in their choices: "Mines a curry"; "I like pasta with cheese."
Resource change	◆ Inclusion of a variety of recipe cards made with children and old recipe books. Put in smaller containers for gathering their own spaces and herbs.

Stage 3. Noticed something; took action; changed resources over a number of days; adult was actively engaging in the area

The next stage in the process of exploring the adult role in planning is included in Table 5.3. As adults, we need to step in and out of the play. Even when we step out of direct interaction with children we are observing and thinking about what we noticed. What worked and what did not? What will you add or take away?

TABLE 5.3 Stage 3 mud kitchen example

Initial Moment	
Mud kitchen initial setup	Variety of sizes and types of pans, cake tins, teapots, cups, bowls, sieves; Tree-stump seats and wooden table; Access to mud
Adult role–during and after session	◆ Observation of how children enter the area—Who? When? ◆ Children's choice of resources- which ones were used confidently/less so? Loved? Curious about? ◆ Listening to language and storylines when the children play ◆ Watch the social dynamics: Are all children gaining access? Who might we need to support to develop confidence? Who needs support to care for the space and resources/materials? ◆ Enter the play and model language and use resources. ◆ Think about what children are interested in/talking about. ◆ Remove/add resources.
Observation summary	The children have been fascinated by the way the water moves objects around the bowl when they stir it.
Adult role	◆ Note down 2 or 3 observations: images (photo and film) and direct speech quotes. ◆ Decide on a dominant aspect—in this case, movement of materials on water. ◆ Collect lightweight resources from the area/home that have a variety to give choice when children use them—inspire curiosity. ◆ Find the larger bowl and put it in an area for children to find. This may help children notice the vortex. ◆ Tidy and set up the area for the next session.

(Continued)

TABLE 5.3 (Continued)

First resource change	
Resource change	Lighter weight materials nearby or in containers to "go shopping"Such as pine needles, dry leaves, fir conesLarger bowls and check access to spoons and sticks
Adult role	◆ Observation of how the children respond to the lightweight materials: Which made them curious? Ask questions? Investigate? ◆ Step in to introduce language, such as *vortex, spiral, stirring around.* ◆ Model "going shopping" to gather materials and take back to the kitchen. ◆ Ask wondering questions: How did that happen? Why? What do you think? ◆ Record the children's responses as documentation of their thinking.
Observation summary	The children discovered some dry dirt underneath the table area and talked about why it was dry. "Let's make it with sprinkles or salt"; "My dad uses spices at home when he cooks tea."

Second resource change	
Resource change	Provision of 3 or 4 containers with dry earth, leaves crumbled up, and out-of-date spices available in the cooking area
Adult role	◆ Share the memory of what was said the day before. ◆ Use children's words and expand on them: "Salt—I use a little bit on my potatoes to make them taste better. There is pink salt in the cupboard called Himalayan salt. It needs a grinder to make the lumps smaller."
Observation summary	A great engagement with the dry materials. Greater cultural engagement in their choices: "Mine's a curry'" "I like pasta with cheese."
Adult role	◆ Observe how children respond to the new materials. ◆ Document their wonderings, theories, and phrases they use. ◆ Hold the memories by writing them up in a learning story to share with other staff and families. ◆ Make links Inside, Outside, and Beyond. Introduce a few salt crystals to explore at group conversation; add a salt production image and a grinder to the Talking Tub.

Third resource change	
Resource change	Create and adapt the Talking Tub about what resources they need in the mud kitchen given the increase in food choices. Collect images and objects that will be familiar and widen their awareness of the natural world.

Table 5.3 shows how much an adult is doing before, during, and after the session with children.

Consider how the adult is actively planning and documenting the learning over several days rather than a series of unconnected activities.

Stage 4. Noticed something; took action; changed resources over a number of days; adult was actively engaging in the area; analysis of the learning

Table 5.4 examines the learning within the experience rather than simply the resources or an activity. The team at Auchlone Nature Kindergarten use Floorbooks™ (Warden, 2012b). Floorbooks are Warden's participatory planning that is built on a number of theoretical concepts and is now used globally to document children's nature-based experiences. In her work on the creation and theorization of nature pedagogy, she suggests that nature pedagogy must embrace planning with and for children rather than adults planning activities without consulting children. Floorbooks are explored more in Chapter 6: "Holder of Memories."

TABLE 5.4 Stage 4 mud kitchen example

Initial Moment	
Mud kitchen initial setup	Variety of sizes and types of pans, cake tins, teapots, cups, bowls, sieves Tree stump seats/wooden table Access to mud
Adult role—during and after session	◆ Observation of how children enter the area: Who? When? ◆ Children's choice of resources: Which ones were used confidently/less so? Loved? Curious about? ◆ Listen to language and storylines when the children play. ◆ Watch the social dynamics: Are all children gaining access? ◆ Enter the play and model language and use resources. ◆ Think about what children are interested in/talking about. ◆ Remove/add resources

(Continued)

TABLE 5.4 (Continued)

Observation summary	The children have been fascinated by the way the water moves objects around the bowl when they stir it
Children's theories and ideas	Water moves. Objects float and some float. Water has power.
Adult role	◆ Note down 2 or 3 observations—images (photo and film) and direct speech quotes. ◆ Decide on a dominant aspect—in this case, movement of materials on water. ◆ Collect lightweight resources from the area/home that have a variety to give choice when children use them—inspire curiosity. ◆ Find the larger bowl and put it in an area for children to find. This may help children notice the vortex. ◆ Tidy and set up the area for the next session.

First resource change

Resource change	Lighter weight materials nearby or in containers to "go shopping," such as pine needles, dry leaves, fir cones Larger bowls and check access to spoons and sticks
Adult role	◆ Observe how the children respond to the lightweight materials: Which made them curious? Ask questions? Investigate? ◆ Step in to introduce language such as *vortex, spiral, stirring around.* ◆ Model "going shopping" to gather materials to take back to the kitchen. ◆ Ask wondering questions: How did that happen? Why? What do you think? ◆ Record the children's responses as documentation of their thinking.
Observation summary	The children discovered some dry dirt underneath the table area and talked about why it was dry: "Let's make it with sprinkles or salt"; "My dad uses spices at home when he cooks tea."
Children's theories and ideas	Earth can be dry or wet. Dry things are used in cooking. There are words like herbs and spaces to describe food.

Second resource change

Resource change	Provision of 3 or 4 containers with dry earth, leaves crumbled up, and out-of-date spices available in the cooking area
Observation summary	A great engagement with the dry materials. Greater cultural engagement in their choices: "Mine's a curry"; "I like pasta with cheese."

(Continued)

TABLE 5.4 (Continued)

Children's theories and ideas	Humans eat a variety of food. My family eats different things to other families. We choose the food we cook and eat.
Adult role	◆ Share the memory of what was said the day before. ◆ Use children's words and expand on them: "Salt—I use a little bit on my potatoes to make them taste better. There is pink salt in the cupboard called Himalayan salt. It needs a grinder to make the lumps smaller." ◆ Document their wonderings, theories, and phrases they use to write up in a Learning story to share with other staff and families.
Third resource change	
Resource change	Create and adapt the Talking Tub about what resources they need in the mud kitchen given the increase in food choices.

In this series of tables, we explore the increasing complexity of what it means to plan for the possibilities that a nature-based environment can offer. Some of the moments that will occur are unpredictable and unique. It is therefore vital that the adult has the confidence in preparation of being the facilitator. Much of the responsive planning requires adults to have vast numbers of experiences up their sleeves so that they can pull one out when required.

WHAT IT SOUNDS LIKE: EXAMPLES OF LANGUAGE RELATED TO PLANNING

Conversations with co-teachers about why we are making different planning decisions ensure that we are all being intentional in our plans. We can also narrate and explain our plans with children so they can see their questions and ideas are valuable. Here are some examples of language we might hear when being intentional about planning for and with children.

Internal language or language with co-teachers

"How can we extend the idea Liam has about where the puddles go?"

"I have noticed some children have a real fascination with building shelters at the moment, has anyone else? I wonder if we can enrich that area?"

"I have a series of images showing Lara being so caring with a worm in the digging zone. How could we use this moment as a springboard for a conversation with the whole group."

"Does anyone have thoughts about how we can support Chris to feel more confident in sharing his ideas with his peers?"

Language to use with children

"Huh. What does that make you wonder about?"

"I heard you say that tomorrow you'd like to build a home for the frog you found. What materials would you like me to have for you tomorrow?"

In this approach, we embrace the idea of planning for the possibilities of play rather than the apparent certainties of adult direction. It follows that the way we then document the learning through nature-based playful inquiries is flexible, dynamic, and consultative. We explore how we document this process in the following chapter.

Self-reflection

♦ Take time to look at your planning and documentation this week.
  ♦ How much is built on children's curiosities?
  ♦ Where have you documented caring behaviors?
  ♦ Are all children represented in the documentation?
  ♦ Do you show a series of photos or just one? If only one, how do you share the growth of perseverance, failure/response, confidence?
♦ Does your planning link experiences Inside, Outside, and Beyond?
♦ Do ideas for experiences come from children or adults? If both, are they balanced?

6

Holder of memories

Documenting children's learning

Throughout Western history, we seem to value what we record. As society moved toward valuing writing and reading more than speaking and listening, the written word became the key focus of education. We have come to understand that we need to redress the balance, especially in the early stages of education, in order to acknowledge the value of speaking and listening in learning we need to record them, and the physicality of learning by doing, in a way that ironically uses images and words.

Documentation allows us to make visible the often transient experiences that take place in a playful environment indoors or outdoors. These can then be used for sharing with children, carers, and families so they are aware of what we do when working with their children. When families see the capacities of children developing and the intention that adults put into creating rich opportunities, it makes conversations easier and more accessible, especially if they are new to nature-based pedagogy. When talking with families about more sensitive areas, such as a lack of care or confidence, documentation helps show a time when they did display those traits, so the conversation starts from a point of achievement rather than a deficit. In this way, we can talk about *building on* and *extending* rather than *needs to be* or *should be*.

DOI: 10.4324/9781003374053-6

Parents and carers are part of the documentation process as we work in partnership. There are many digital platforms and strategies to help this, all of which provide another perspective. The same content can then be used with colleagues to discuss the theories and ideas that children share across the center or age groups. Through this activity, the whole team is aware of the learning, and it does not rest on a single person but a group. This is key to ensure that if there is staff absence, there are others who know how to take the learning forward rather than it stopping. Using the skills and talents of a group of colleagues is enriching as it draws on multiple perspectives to understand what the child is doing, not just one. Learning how to learn is referred to as metacognition and strategies that we use are more important for lifelong learning than just relying on children gathering knowledge. Let us look at an example of the journey of the purpose of documentation linked to the unplanned experience of finding a feather.

Children build up theories and patterns of understanding of the world around them from birth. The encounters they have and the interactions with adults allow the brain to make connections and build an awareness of concepts, skills, and knowledge. Here, we use a found material—a feather. Imagine that the child reaches for a feather on the ground; the first encounter may just be to hold it and the sense of its shape and weight; the next might be to look at the feather's edge and feel how soft it is; the adult interacts to use key descriptive language, such as *feather*, *light*, *soft*, *edge*; the child leaves the feather and moves onto something else. In the revisiting, perhaps some days later, some of the experience is still there as a trace in the child's mind, and so behaviors are repeated. The adult uses language again: "Do you remember we found a feather a few days ago? It was so light, and you noticed the edge was soft." At this point, a process of myelination occurs along the neural pathway as the child repeats, albeit in a slightly different form, awareness of what a feather is. This spiraling around and around a single material, such as a feather, deepens awareness. Our role as adults is to be aware of the possibilities (as discussed in the planning chapter) and step in and out of the experiences to extend or challenge children's thinking, helping them find strategies to observe, research, make connections between, and explain what they think. Consider how revisiting something as simple as a feather over time can help children explore concepts of variety and complexity, color, mass, form, movement, origin, and quantity. Warden (2020) refers to these as lines of inquiry that run through long-term documentation in her approach to planning and documentation called Floorbooks. By looking at these larger concepts rather than stand-alone experiences, we help all children understand how to observe, how to find out more, and how to adjust your thinking over time.

Documentation is the recording of these encounters in a variety of ways so that all children are able to share what they know. In a simplified way, what children have said is speaking and listening, images of what they did share physical knowledge and drawings, and emergent writing of their thoughts embraces writing. Encouraging children to share what they know in many different ways and supporting adults in realizing this complexity were made more accessible in early childhood through the work of Loris Malaguzzi and the teachers of Reggio Emelia in Italy. He used the phrase "one hundred languages of children" to help adults transition from the narrowness of writing to embracing all the different ways humans can share what they know.

The complexity of this style of documentation comes when you involve adult voices in terms of analysis, reflection, and the creation of the next steps in the spiral mentioned earlier. It moves the collection of pictures and words into a form that supports teacher dialogue. Dialogue here is seen as more than a chat as it requires analysis, an exchange of ideas to consider what children were exploring. Warden (2020) refers to these next steps created after dialogue as a team as possible lines of development (PLODs). The ideas for experiences created by adults (in response to children's theories) are noted in the documentation alongside the images and voices of the children rather than only in a planning journal. They remain as possibilities as they cannot always be guaranteed to happen; when they do, they are ticked and dated in the Floorbook to demonstrate action. It is at this point that they appear in a planning journal as an experience to take place that day or week (Figure 6.1).

FIGURE 6.1 Adult completing a Floorbook with children.

Outdoor documentation

Being outside offers some additional challenges from the weather, but the majority of the time, these aspects are the same Inside, Outside, or Beyond.

- **Take photographs** of the process of play not a single shot but multiple to show the series of things the children did to create a story.
- Create a **documentation board** in an area that families will see. In an outdoor kindergarten, this may be wrapped around a tree or outside a shelter.
- Create spaces for children to put their **own displays** and discoveries.
- Use **film clips** to share the dynamic way play evolves in nature-based environments.
- **Give children the camera to record** something that they wish to explore further when in another space such as inside or vice versa.

- ◆ Use **small field journals** that can move easily across locations in a backpack.
- ◆ Take **photographs with children** of the traces left behind after their play, such as a den in the forest, a mud cake, an ice tower, or a mud creature on a tree.
- ◆ Use an adult hip belt with a **notepad** to access quickly so that quotes of what children say can be easily recorded and used later to share the memory.

Documenting curiosity, confidence, and care

In relation to documenting curiosity, confidence, and care, we need to dig a little deeper to consider how we can make them more tangible or observable in our documentation. Let us consider the features that are required in any planning and documentation approach rooted in nature pedagogy when it values being curious so that children develop confidence and care for the natural world.

- ◆ **Centered on children's curiosities**. This could be a dead mouse, a bone, the way the wind moves the leaves, the shadows on the floor, the way a fish moves in a tank, or a leaf forming on a houseplant. The joy of this way of working is the unpredictability of what the natural world will offer us irrespective of the location. The adult role here is to notice, consider, and respond in a way that gives value to being curious, no question or observation is rejected.
- ◆ **Accessible for children to look at**. The affirmation, or feedback loop, that children receive when they look back at their learning is key to developing a sense of confidence. The documentation of the words they said provides value to their opinion; images of them having a go at a new task demonstrates commitment; an image of several design attempts of a boat demonstrates perseverance; and an image of their physical growth and its associated skills demonstrates how they are becoming more capable.

◆ **Links experiences between school and home**. Documenting experiences allows children to make connections across the many places they encounter such as school and home. When the significant people in their lives help children make these linkages explicit, it is easier for them to make sense of their world, ask questions, build their ideas, and know what action to take next.

◆ **Works in nature time**. Developing care takes time and rather than there being a single moment where it is achieved, it is built up through hundreds of tiny moments. This is what we refer to as "nature time" (Warden, 2015). Documentation therefore needs to collate these memories of actions that took place. These small moments build up to tell a story and the small changes in curiosity, confidence, and care can become more visible.

◆ **Collates evidence of nature time in other people meaningful to children**. Building on the idea of nature time, some aspects of documentation run across families and generations. In many communities, a family's commitment to models of early education, such as nature kindergartens, nature preschools, forest schools, and the like, means that several children from one family may join the program over time. Imagine then the idea that children can look back at the adventures of their siblings, cousins, or perhaps even parents playing in the same spaces. The use of the capacity of digital storage or indeed library areas means that we can support this intergenerational connection.

Quality documentation

This requires adults in the space to have a clear focus and apply effort to their role. As with all aspects of our professionalism, the more effort we apply the more likely it is that we will improve quality. Table 6.1 provides some tasks that adults need to think about and do every day if they are to be effective in their documentation.

TABLE 6.1 Teacher role, actions, and purpose in quality documentation

Role	What?	So what?
Prepare	Check work box has ◆ paper for recording/ drawing ◆ pens that work The group area in the room is tidy or a mat for outside Charged camera	Having materials to hand keeps children engaged more effectively than getting up during group time. Children need to be able to hear each other or you when you ask what they think. Technology can only help when it works.
Arrange	Which adults are actively observing, and which have the overview of the group?	It is impossible to focus on documenting learning if you are also trying to do supervision of a large number of children.
Notice	Look at the children and have a clear set of questions in your head. Who? What are they doing/talking about? Where? When?	It is tempting to look at and not notice by skimming past what children are doing too quickly/
Slow down	Experiences	Some children have a tendency to rush through tasks and experiences. It is an intentional moment for the adult to stop and say let us take some time to do this.
Explain	What you are doing, and why?	We expect children to know what we are doing and why. Explaining who it is for and what you are saying about their work can be shared.
Ask	Ask if you can take their photograph/film them.	Children have a right not to be photographed. Withdrawing consent can sometimes be by turning away.
	Ask if you can enter the play such as a den or fort.	It is polite and respectful to ask before you march into an area created by children.
Listen	Listen to the conversation and note key phrases in a notebook or on a device.	Adults do not always need to speak; listening can give a better insight than questioning.

(Continued)

TABLE 6.1 (Continued)

Role	What?	So what?
Question sensitively	Ask clarifying questions to help you understand their thinking. Try to not ask too many questions.	Adults have power in a child's eyes and the presence of the adult can stop or redirect the play.
Offer	Offer the camera to the children for them to take the images or the film.	Many children are capable of using technology. This provides the agency and empowerment that will allow you to see it through their eyes.
Reflect on the event/ experience	Why did it happen? What went before? What came after? What went well?	Reflection is often linked to the experience itself and allows us to learn from experience.
Research	Knowledge, concepts, and skills that may be useful to take the learning forward	Nobody knows everything. Children will ask a question that you cannot answer to let them see you research with them.
Engage in reflexivity	Of your own behavior. What did you say? What impact did that have? How could you have changed what you did? How did you feel?	Reflexivity is thinking about your role in the experience and is key to your self-improvement.

It is apparent from the table that many aspects of documentation have to come together for it to be effective even at the point before you share it with families. A single image on a random bit of paper couldn't really be described as quality, so what is? Let us use Floorbooks as an example.

Floorbooks as an approach to documentation

As mentioned earlier, one planning and documentation approach is called Floorbooks. Figure 6.2 provides a sample page from a Floorbook. Floorbooks are an integral part of Warden's work on nature pedagogy as demonstrated in *Learning with Nature—Embedding Outdoor Practice* (2015) and *Green Teaching—Nature Pedagogies for Climate Change and Sustainability* (2022).

FIGURE 6.2 A page from a Floorbook.

A Floorbook is not a scrapbook. Rather, it is a form of documentation that requires a high level of analysis by adults. A quick summary follows:

- ◆ Documentation that is current and up to date as it is used daily
- ◆ Content that is relevant to children
- ◆ Pictures cut out by both children and adults
- ◆ Space between pictures for the children to draw and write
- ◆ Pages dated to show a chronology and pacing of children's learning
- ◆ An overview called the learning Journey at the rear of the book to show the lines the Inquiry the play explored
- ◆ Adult creates next steps (PLODs) in the Floorbook
- ◆ PLODs ticked and dated when used in planning—there should then be evidence in the Floorbook of how that took place
- ◆ The voice of the child, family, and adults are all in the Floorbook

WHAT IT SOUNDS LIKE: EXAMPLES OF
LANGUAGE RELATED TO DOCUMENTATION

By holding children's memories for them and re-presenting them at another time, we can develop their sense of confidence in their own ideas. They can then revisit these memories many times. Documenting the ways children are curious and caring also sends a message to children that we as adults value them are their ideas. We can narrate what we do when we are documenting children's thinking so that children are clear as to the purpose. Here are some examples of language we might use when being intentional about documenting with children:

Internal language or language with co-teachers

"How can we ensure that taking pictures and video isn't taking away some of the wonderful moments we have?"

"The experience we planned for around entrapment in the ice has provided some fascinating theories about how ice and water are related. Please share any thoughts and feedback with me so we can create more detail in the Floorbook and in the group learning story."

"I have a series of images showing Ella being so caring with a worm in the digging zone. How could we use this moment as a springboard for a conversation with the whole group."

"Has anyone gathered any images or words from Emily? There is a wonderful learning story about her love and care for the potatoes, and I would like to widen it to show her care of other things?"

Language to use with children

"How can we remember to investigate that when we are back at base camp? Do you think writing it down might help?

"Is it OK if I take your photograph, then we can look at it later or share with your family?"

"Let me write down what you are thinking. It is such an interesting idea. What shall we do next? Do you need any suggestions from me?"

While looking back at the documentation, "Let me read these words to you. Elizabeth said that she thought the little beetle needed to be somewhere quiet and damp. How caring. Any other ideas of how we can care for beetles?"

When looking at your documentation it is important to consider who the audience is. In Floorbooks, children are first, then families, and, finally, staff. This evidence is also useful for Licensing or other regulators. However, if your purpose is to provide evidence of what you did for licensing, it may look and be used in a different way.

Self-reflection

♦ Take time to look at your documentation this week:
  ♦ How are children involved?
  ♦ Where have you documented caring behaviors?
  ♦ Are all children represented in the documentation, or are the confident children the ones who seem to appear in front of your camera?
  ♦ Do you show a series of photos or just one? If only one, how do you share the growth of perseverance, failure/response, confidence?
♦ Do you only document what you plan? Or do you document significant moments planned or not?
♦ How do you manage the balance of digital and hard copy documentation? What are the benefits of both?

7

Relationship builder

With self and others

Nature-based pedagogy is an approach to working with children that makes explicit and develops our relationship with the natural world (Warden, 2022; Larimore, 2019). As Claire mentioned in her book: "Nature pedagogy has become a way of being with nature that puts the natural world at the heart of its philosophy, and practice through a relational worldview that embraces the observable and unobservable worlds of living and non-living elements" (Warden, 2022, p. 34).

Educators help children to build relationships with themselves and others. "Others" includes their peers, adults, and the natural world—both living and nonliving things. All of these relationships—with themselves, others, and the natural world—are foundational to children's development of curiosity, confidence, and care. Relationships are all about connection and reciprocity. In interpersonal relationships, feeling valued, seen, and heard is what leads to a feeling of connection. We also must treat others in a way that they also feel connected. Similarly, in relationship with the natural world, we receive many gifts from the natural world (air, water, space, moments of awe, etc.), but we also have a responsibility to take care of the natural world. As Robin Wall Kimmerer wisely said in *Braiding Sweetgrass* about relationships:

DOI: 10.4324/9781003374053-7

Each person, human or no, is bound to every other in a reciprocal relationship. Just as all beings have a duty to me, I have a duty to them. If an animal gives its life to feed me, I am in turn bound to support its life. If I receive a stream's gift of pure water, then I am responsible for returning a gift in kind. An integral part of a human's education is to know those duties and how to perform them.

(p. 115)

In nature-based pedagogy, we have two terms that are particularly relevant here. First, related to pedagogy, or the process of teaching, we talk about the concept of "learning *with* nature." Learning *with* nature means learning that emerges from experiences with nature, relies on the natural world as another teacher, and then leads to additional learning through a reciprocal relationship (Warden, 2015; Larimore 2019; Bailie, Larimore, and Pikus, 2023). This approach leads to learning that is meaningful to the individual child and results in both cognitive and emotional connections (Bailie, Larimore, and Pikus, 2023).

Second, the desired outcome of nature-based pedagogy is often talked about as education for the planet, people, and community (Warden, 2015; Larimore 2019; Bailie, Larimore, and Pikus, 2023). A phrase for this is "learning *for* nature" which recognizes the reciprocity with nature we discussed earlier (Fox et al., 2021).

Relationships Inside, Outside, and Beyond

Throughout this book, we've talked about the Inside, Outside, and Beyond. Primarily, the focus of these three terms is on physical learning spaces. However, as we mentioned in the Introduction and "What Is Nature Pedagogy?" (Chapter 1), we also think of the Inside, Outside, and Beyond as a *relational* metaphor for social-emotional learning.

We have both been thinking and talking about this metaphor extensively. Yes, we both see the "Inside, Outside, and Beyond" not only as physical spaces but also as a relational way of being in those spaces. We see the Inside as our individual, internal world; the Outside as our relationships with people and the planet; and the Beyond as our relationships with the global community as well as the unobservable aspects of life. As educators our role as "relationship builders" includes encouraging children's relationship with the Inside, Outside, and Beyond, that is, with themselves, other people, their local place, and something bigger than themselves.

Inside: Relationships with self

Being in a relationship with oneself includes self-awareness of our own thoughts, feelings, and behaviors. Relationship with self not only includes self-awareness but also self-care and nurturing, that is, not only recognizing one's own needs but also working to meet those needs. We can do this by taking action ourselves, asking others for help, setting boundaries to protect our needs, and so forth. In early childhood, young children are still learning how to recognize their own feelings and thoughts. They are also learning what are and are not appropriate behaviors in response to those thoughts and feelings. Our role as educators is to help them in the learning process.

In the early years, we spend a lot of time helping children see how they are feeling and what they can do to solve their problem, for example, a young child crying because their hands are cold and wet after sticking them in a puddle or a child is frustrated because they want to keep playing but it's time to go to lunch.

In fact, almost always what we label as a "behavioral issue" is actually an expression of a child's unmet need that they may or may not be aware of and/or able to verbally express. That's why our role as a relationship builder is so vital for children's individual success. We must be observant of children's verbal and nonverbal communication, what is happening in the moments leading up to that communication, and what unmet needs they may be expressing. Then, our job is to not only help children recognize and articulate that need but also take steps to meet their needs.

Children's needs come in many forms. Their needs might be related to their physical comfort. They might, for example, be hot, have a scratchy tag that's bugging them, be hungry, and so forth. Children also have a variety of social-emotional needs. For example, a child might be frustrated that they can't see the story the teacher is reading during group time. They might also be feeling a lack of connection with others—left out, isolated, not heard, not valued, and the like.

In a moment, we'll talk more about relationships with others—particularly asking for what we need from adults and problem-solving with their peers. Core to these relationships and problem-solving in those relationships, however, is children having self-awareness of their own feelings and needs. This is one of the reasons why programs like Conscious Discipline include identifying feelings in the problem-solving process—to become attuned to one's own emotions and needs.

The role of relationship builder with self can seem daunting, but in many ways, it's what early childhood educators do every day. We're helping them to not only navigate their own thoughts, feelings, and behaviors to be content within their own minds and hearts but also have relationships with those outside of themselves.

Outside: Relationships with others and the natural world

In addition to supporting children's relationship with themselves, nature-based early childhood educators also play a role in helping children build relationships with others. This includes other children, adults, and the natural world.

When it comes to building relationships with others, we can help children see how others are similar to us in terms of identity, interests, wants, and needs. However, it's in the early years that children are learning that other people may have different perspectives than their own. We talked earlier about labeling feelings during problem-solving to help children identify their own needs. Labeling feelings in the problem-solving process also helps children see that others may have different perspectives. For example, we can help children see that they both wanted to play with the materials, but when I shoved them to get it, I hurt the other child's body and feelings. We can then help children see other ways they may ask for or negotiate with someone else to find a compromise.

Teacher–child interactions throughout the class day help children to develop relationships with not only other children but also with adults. We support them to connect with adults to not only ask for what they need but also build more personal attachments. Sharing stories, telling jokes, and listening to one another builds a relationship and connection between the child and adult where they feel individually valued, seen, and heard.

Additionally, as educators, we can facilitate children's relationship with the natural world. We first do this through the various other roles discussed in this book such as providing time, materials, and experiences. Specific to relationship building, however, we can help make explicit the feelings and connections children may be developing with nature. If, for example, we see a child admiring a flower we might give them space to observe and then when they've finished say something like "You were really admiring that flower. It seems pretty special to you. How do you feel now that you've admired it?" Or perhaps, over the course of the week, children have been noticing squirrel tracks in the snow around a tree and begin telling a story about what animal it is and what it's been doing. We can encourage that storytelling with questions like "What do you think we'll see today when we go visit the tree where the squirrel tracks have been?"

When it comes to supporting children's relationships with others, we can be aware of what researchers John and Julie Gottman of the Gottman Institute call "bids for connections." They describe a bid for connection as an expression of wanting to feel emotionally connected to someone else. These bids for connection can be nonverbal or verbal and are ways children ask to connect with someone or something. For example, nonverbally, we might see a child reach out to touch something in nature, reach out and hug another child, or lean into a teacher's side while listening to a story. Verbally, a bid for connection may sound like a question but may also be a comment such as "Whoa, that bird is big!" That is an opportunity for us as adults to respond to someone, so the child knows they were heard and what they have to say is valued. The level of response may be a simple acknowledgment like "You saw a big bird?" or more involved such as "Wow! You're right that bird is big. I wonder what kind of bird it is. Do you have any ideas?" This more involved response may, in turn, lead to a conversation during which there are multiple turns in talk between the adult and child on the same topic (Cabell et al., 2015; De Rivera et al., 2005; Larimore, 2021).

Beyond: Relationships with something bigger than themselves

In nature-based education, we often talk about the power of experiences in nature to provide us with awe, wonder, and joy. These are feelings that are often much too difficult to describe in words, with words rarely capturing the depth and detail of the feelings themselves. These feelings are part of spiritual development. Spirituality is about the human spirit and the notion that there is something bigger than ourselves that connects us with other people and the natural world. To be clear, we are not talking about a belief or thought (i.e., religion) but, rather, the emotions that connect us. In her book *Nature and Young Children*, Ruth Wilson (2012) explained, "Spirituality is more aligned with 'spirit' than with 'belief.' Spirit is the vital principle or animating force within living things. Spirituality puts us in touch with this force" (p. 69).

Talk of children's development has virtually ignored the idea of "spiritual development." This is likely, at least in part, due to the concerns over this being confused with religious education. Yet, there is growing evidence that children have inherent spiritual capacities (e.g., Hart, 2005; Miller, 2015). We can support spiritual development in the early years by facilitating children's mindfulness as they navigate the world. Deborah Schein (2018), a researcher of young children's spirituality, explained:

> The spiritual aspect of mindfulness and mindsight is that humans are capable of having these very deep, significant feelings. These feelings touch our inner self, our essences, or our dispositions and help us to integrate our body, mind, and spirit.
>
> (p. 79)

The natural world provides opportunities for children to experience awe and wonder and integrate their bodies, minds, and spirits. Schein (2014) described the power of nature for spiritual development when she said,

> It nurtures our spiritual side—our sense of self, our basic dispositions of wonderment and joy, and our complex dispositions of caring, kindness, empathy, and reverence that are capable of guiding us to becoming kinder human beings, thus creating a better world.
>
> (p. 94)

As nature-based educators we can support children's connection with the natural world and spiritual development by providing opportunities for awe and wonder. We can also be intentional about allowing children the space to feel those moments while remaining silent—we don't have to narrate every experience. We may choose to discuss it later, but in the moment, we can allow the space to feel. For example, if children are watching a dragonfly emerge out of his nymph casing, a simple "Wow!" followed by silence may be all the language needed. We can then allow the child to decide when they're ready to ask questions or reflect on the experience.

Another important factor for nature-based educators to keep in mind when thinking about spiritual development is recognizing relationships with the natural world develop over time. For example, regular visits to the same place in the natural world over many seasons will help children see the subtle shifts in the seasons and the small moments of awe and wonder that happen every day.

Schein (2018) summed up the importance of our role in spiritual development when she said,

> When we address spiritual development, we look at the deepest reasons for why humans need nature. Being in nature also provides us with an ability to become peaceful cohabitants of the earth. To provide these moments for young children, we must pay closer attention to the kind of environments we are providing.
>
> (p. 88)

Caring for children is foundational to relationship building

One way we begin to develop children's relationships with themselves, the outer world, and the world beyond is to model positive relationships by caring for them. Often, education in the early years is referred to as care *and* education. In 2021, Carol Garboden Murray published *Illuminating Care: The Pedagogy and Practice of Care in Early Childhood and Communities*, which is rooted in the idea that care and education are not separate concepts but, rather, that care *is* education. Murray said, "Care is not subordinate to education, care is education. When we unite care and education, we care in a way that nurtures another's independence, actualization, and self-sufficiency" (pp. 23–24). In other words, care is a vital component in education, and we also contend it supports the development of care as a human skill in the children we care for. In caring for children when they're young, we are also supporting their ability to care for themselves, other people, and the planet.

All early childhood programs care for children during meals and snacks, rest time, toileting, and when attending to injury. In nature-based settings, moments of care are often even more common due to outdoor hazards such as weather, topography, plants, animals, and risky play. For example, in nature-based settings where children spend large portions of the day outside, we are constantly aware of how dry or warm children are. There may also be moments of care related to riskier activities such as stick play, being around campfires, climbing trees, and so forth. By attending to children's physical and emotional needs in these situations we are building connections and relationships between adults and children.

We're helping them tune into their own bodies and what actions they can take to care for themselves. In caring for children and our classroom, we're also modeling for them how to care for the world around them—other people, our classroom spaces, nature, and so forth.

WHAT IT SOUNDS LIKE: EXAMPLES OF LANGUAGE RELATED TO BUILDING RELATIONSHIPS

There are many types of relationships that we have, all of them require effort to maintain them. A key aspect in supporting the development of curious, confident, and caring children is that we need to narrate our actions a little more; this applies to conversations as well as tangible things like providing resources. This makes the behavior more defined, and in that way, we would suggest it is easier for children to replicate. An easily accessible moment is when we care for children gives us the daily opportunity to explain why we are doing certain things. These moments also help teach children how to take care of their own needs and develop a relationship with self. Here are some examples of language we might use when being intentional about building relationships.

Internal language or language with co-teachers

"It is wonderful to see how Devon and Ryan have developed a tolerance of each other. The next stage may be some facilitated play together."

"How can we slow down the walk to the forest to allow for some dawdling and meandering? It feels like a march and we are missing so many of the curious things along the path."

"I wonder if we need to teach some strategies for entering the play. Darren spent a long time building the den, so perhaps the other children need to offer something to contribute rather than expecting to just go in and take over?"

Language to use with children

"Your hands look really red, are they cold? Would you like to wear these gloves?"

"It is so wonderful to go slowly like Emma; she sees much more than me. I am going to go slowly and see what I can see along the path."

"Isn't it a wonderful thing when someone is listening and looking at you? It makes me feel like they care—how about you?"

"It is OK to feel angry; it will pass. When it does, perhaps you can help us work on making the model together. We are looking forward to being with you."

Self-reflection

♦ Take time to think about a relationship you have:
  ♦ Do both sides care? If it's an object, how do you care for it?
  ♦ What time and effort do you put into nurturing it?
  ♦ What phrases do you use to help children develop social skills? Are they positive and affirming?
  ♦ In your interactions do you give a solution or make statements such as "play nicely"?
♦ How do you view your relationship with children? Do they feel able to approach you?
♦ To what extent do you feel it is not your role to share your experiences with children?

8

Conversationalist

In the previous chapter, we explored the role of relationship builder. While there are many aspects to relationship building, you may have noticed one essential aspect is engaging in conversation. Not only are conversations important for relationship building (i.e., social-emotional development), but they're also important for developing thoughts and ideas (i.e., cognitive development). That is why we include being a conversationalist and encouraging dialogue around thoughts and ideas as another essential role of the nature pedagogue.

Conversations are different from simply expressing an idea or asking a question. Instead, conversations are a responsive discussion—they clarify for understanding and build on each other's thoughts and ideas. Research has shown that preschool teachers generally use statements more than questions, particularly cognitively challenging questions, in their interactions with children (Massey et al., 2008; Tu & Hsiao, 2008; Chen & de Groot, 2014; Leuchter et al., 2020). Yet a responsive discussion includes multiple turns in talk on the same general topic based on deep listening and thoughtful, connected responses. This is very different from asking a question and walking away. It's also very different from telling a child a bit of information or even telling a child what to do or not do related to behavior management and rules. Rather, conversations build an emotional connection while also exploring ideas and thoughts intellectually.

DOI: 10.4324/9781003374053-8

Studies have also shown that where and when those interactions occur influences the ways interactions unfold (e.g., Cabell et al., 2015; De Rivera et al., 2005; Larimore, 2021). Particularly related to nature-based pedagogy, Larimore (2021) found that the longest conversations between teachers and children occurred during free choice and were generally impromptu, child-led, and in small-group interactions. The same study found that longer interactions tended to occur outdoors with more physical and metaphorical space. The outdoors also provided more things to talk about than the indoor space—such as birds flying by, a worm on the ground, or a flower blooming. All this to say, we as educators have great influence over how conversations emerge and the quality of those conversations.

There are a few ways being a conversationalist comes to life in the classroom. The most obvious way is to engage in conversation with children directly. We can also encourage conversations among children, and we can model conversations with our co-teachers. Whether it is a teacher–child, child–child, or teacher–teacher conversation, all conversations are influenced by the types of questions and statements, emotional affect, and physicality.

Questions and statements within a conversation

As we said before, conversations should be a back-and-forth interaction where two or more people are deeply listening and then responding to one another's ideas. The back-and-forth exchanges happen through questions and statements. We recognize that many education books have been written about questions and prompts. Our goal here is not to reiterate the types of questions and prompts so much as why and how those prompts are useful in developing conversations rather than disjointed statements of language.

First, the different types of prompts in interactions. We can ask questions that are either closed-ended or open-ended. Close-ended questions are those that prompt a clear answer such as yes/no, color, size, and so on. Whereas open-ended questions allow for a broader range of responses. For example, when look-ing at a flower, asking, "What color is that?" is a closed-ended question, whereas asking, "Why do you think it's folded up like that?" is an open-ended question. We can also prompt interac-tions through statements. Statements are phrases that aren't directly asking a question. Statements vary in how much they suggest an invitation for the other person to elaborate. For exam-ple, a declarative statement such as "That's red" isn't implying a question but might elicit a response if the other person dis-agrees and thinks the point is worthy of discussion. Other state-ments, such as "I wonder what that bird is trying to say with its song," provide more opportunity for others to elaborate without directly asking the question.

So what role do these different types of prompts play in con-versation? Generally speaking, open-ended questions require higher order thinking skills to respond. The answers to open-ended questions are also more likely to provide something inter-esting for someone else to respond to. Along those same lines, statements provide an opening for someone else to share their ideas and thoughts in response to the statement without asking a direct question. This is similar to the bids for connection we dis-cussed in the relationship-building chapter—there's space for the participants to connect intellectually and emotionally with one another. In Table 8.1, we provided specific examples of questions and statements that might deepen and extend a conversation as well as those that might encourage engagement with others.

In addition to *how* we engage children in conversation (i.e., questions or statements), our role as conversationalists also includes considering *what* we are saying. That is, what concepts or ideas are we drawing children's attention to? What range and quality of language are we using in our interactions?

The content of conversations can explore a range of topics related to feelings and thoughts. We can express how we're feel-ing in a given moment or how we felt during a previous experi-ence. We can also explore thoughts on topics related to science, art, language, math, culture, and history. Whether emotional or intellectual ideas, we can explore concepts at a range of depth and with different purposes—many of which are explored in

TABLE 8.1 Questioning prompts

Prompt	Example questions	Example statements
Prompts to deepen and extend conversation	◆ So are you saying …? ◆ What happens if … ◆ What do you notice? ◆ What ideas do you have about …? ◆ Why do you think that? ◆ How do you know? ◆ What does it remind you of?	◆ I wonder … ◆ I was thinking … ◆ It reminds me of …
Prompts to engage with others	◆ Oh, did you hear what they said? ◆ Do you agree with what so-and-so said? ◆ What do you think about that idea? ◆ What do you think they are saying? ◆ Why do you think …? ◆ Can you say more about that?	◆ Tell us more … ◆ Oh, it sounds like …

other chapters in this book. For example, a conversation might relate to our relationships with other people as discussed in Chapter 7 or related to risk management as in Chapter 9.

No matter the topic of conversation and whether we're using questions or statements, we can also expose children to a range of language in conversation. Research is clear that early childhood programs that build conceptual knowledge and vocabulary through language have a significant positive impact on children's reading and comprehension skills down the road (Dickinson, Golinkoff, and Hirsh-Pasek, 2010). So when we're engaging in conversation, using a variety of vocabulary is not only OK but also encouraged. Even shifting simple statements while observing a butterfly—for example, "Oh, that butterfly is coming out!" to "Whoa, that butterfly is emerging out of its chrysalis!"—provide richer vocabulary that is rooted in context. Context is important. We are not suggesting we teach children vocabulary for the sake of knowing words but rather to provide a range of vocabulary for children to make sense of their experiences. This gives the vocabulary context-based, personal meaning.

This context-based vocabulary and language development relates directly to the concept of learning *with* nature in nature-based pedagogy. When the natural world provides an experience, we can then have a conversation to make sense of what we have seen or felt. The experience comes first; then children make observations or ask questions about that experience. Conversations are a vital part of that sensemaking process.

Affect during conversation

The words we use in conversations are clearly very important. However, other factors influence the likelihood that interactions will build into a meaningful, multiturn conversation. Broadly, these factors can be described as "affect" and generally convey emotion through tone, facial expressions, posture, and so forth.

Emotion and tone of voice

We've all experienced moments where the person we're talking to doesn't seem to be listening. Or they seem annoyed with us. What happens? We shut down, right? Emotionally, it feels like "This person doesn't care what I have to say." In contrast, when someone seems genuinely interested in our thoughts and feelings, we want to keep engaging in the conversation, right? We feel valued and heard. We feel connected. The same is true for young children. Part of our role as a conversationalist is to make children feel their ideas matter. There are a few ways we can emotionally connect in conversations.

First, it's important for us as adults to be willing to share our own perspectives in conversation. Connection is a back-and-forth, reciprocal relationship. While being listened to is great, it's also important to feel that sense of trust when someone shares— to be a listener. We're not suggesting you pour your deepest, darkest secrets out. There still need to be appropriate boundaries. But there is value in sharing our experiences, uncertainties, and other thoughts and feelings. For example, a nature-based educator might honestly share, "Snakes make me a little uncomfortable. I know there's nothing to be scared of, but I still get butterflies in my belly when I see one. That's why Teacher Amy held it for me so I could touch it."

Another way we can emotionally connect in conversations with young children is by showing interest in the child. We can do this through the types of questions we ask, the way we position our body, and our tone of voice. The tone of voice sends a particularly strong emotional message. If we have a sharp, forceful tone they may think we're angry. If we have a quiet, calm tone, they may feel we are taking time to listen. If, in response to a child's statement, we simply repeat back, or parrot, what a child has said, they may feel dismissed. For example, if the child says, "Look, Teacher, I found a frog," and we respond with a flat tone of voice "Yes, you found a frog" that may not convey the message that we want to hear more. However, if we say with an excited tone, "Oh, wow. What a huge frog! How did you catch that?" we are extending an invitation to the child to tell us more about the frog, their experience catching it, and what they're noticing now.

All of this to say that in conversation our aim is to convey an open, welcoming tone—that we're interested, curious, hoping to hear more about what the child has to say, and ultimately wanting to build relationships with the child(ren).

Physicality

Tone of voice is one way we express emotion during conversation, but so is the way we move our body. Our facial expressions, gestures, and body positioning also convey emotion. You've probably heard the classic example that standing with feet shoulder width apart and arms crossed shows people we are angry or closed off to emotional connection. That is true, and there are also even more subtle expressions that send a message. A scowl, raised eyebrows, or looking away while people are talking all convey our feelings about the person speaking and what they're sharing.

As much as possible we want to be emotionally present in conversation with children so they feel valued and heard—so they feel connected with a sense of belonging in the learning environment. We can do this by looking at and making eye contact with children as they speak. This shows we are focused on what they're saying. (This is a vital part of deep listening, which we'll explore in a moment.) We should note here that not all children like to make eye contact. We are not suggesting forcing the child to make eye contact. Rather, we are suggesting that adults focus on looking at the child and making the child feel comfortable and heard.

In addition to eye contact, the way we hold our body is important. As we mentioned, folded arms convey a closed-off stance, whereas opening our body suggests we're more open to conversation. In conversation, we also want to be conscious of how we're positioning ourselves in relation to the speaker. Sometimes, we will want to face the child directly. Whereas other times it may be more comfortable, align with the flow and topic of the conversation, or the relationship between the speakers to be side by side. Each situation will be different, and ultimately, our goal is to make children feel we care and are curious about their ideas to help them feel connected and ultimately confident in their own identity.

Deep listening

In our role of engaging with and facilitating conversation, we have to listen to what is being said. We also have to listen for what is being implied and what is *not* being said—all with the goal of understanding the *meaning* of what is being said. Taken together, this is deep listening, that is, listening that focuses on the language and affect in a conversation to understand what thoughts or ideas a child is trying to express.

Not all conversations are verbal

Part of deep listening is also recognizing and embodying the idea that not all conversations have to be verbal. If we notice a child has paused, crouched down, and is carefully observing an ant crawling along a log, we can immediately sense the child's interest. We might, in turn, crouch beside the child without saying a word. Then if the child puts a small rock in front of the ant, we can infer the child is testing whether the ant will stop or go in a different direction. Once the ant has passed the rock, we might in turn place a leaf in front of the ant, nonverbally indicating that we also notice the ant and understand the child is wanting to investigate the ant's behavior. This interaction is only possible by paying close attention and then matching the child's affect and interests.

This sort of nonverbal conversation also supports many of our other roles as educators. For example, it supports building children's relationships with themselves, others, and the natural world. It also requires us to lean into the role of providing time and space.

WHAT IT SOUNDS LIKE: EXAMPLES OF LANGUAGE RELATED TO CONVERSATION

Conversations are balanced exchanges of ideas and thoughts. Each respecting the other's time to speak and responding to the ideas that are said. Here are some examples of language we might use when creating conversations.

Internal language or language with co-teachers

When reflecting on facilitating conversations with and among children

"I have been working with Lara on her listening and responding. It seems that she feels unable to state what she thinks. How could we help her feel her ideas are valued?"

"The use of eye contact and active listening really helped today as we sat in a circle rather than as a large group facing the front."

When modeling quality conversations

"That is a really interesting perspective, mine is slightly different."

"Thank you for giving me the time to share my ideas, it is so much better when we can have a conversation. I am looking forward to hearing your ideas."

Language to use with children

"Can we come and play with you? You have made that water run work in an interesting way. Can you explain it to us and then maybe we could share some ideas and play with you?"

"Having a chat is when we each say what we think; sometimes it is hard to not talk all at once, but if we do that, we cannot hear each other."

"I am really interested to hear more about your dog, and maybe I can tell you about mine?"

"Listening can be really hard work as you have to stop your mind from wandering off. I think it takes practice?"

"Do you prefer it when we sit down and talk or stand up?"

"I just need to take my sunglasses off so that we can look at each other."

Self-reflection

◆ Take time to record a conversation you have with a child or children. Placing the recording in the center will allow you to hear how you actually respond in conversations. A video recording will also allow you to see your body positioning:

  ◆ Did you notice if one person speaks more than the others?
  ◆ Were there any repeated words or phrases that you heard? (Often, management talk can dominate a conversation.)
  ◆ How were you positioning your body during the conversation?
  ◆ How was the child holding their body as you conversed?
  ◆ Could you hear what people were saying? (Many children struggle indoors with rebounded noise.)
  ◆ What was the general noise level like?
  ◆ How do you see the ideas of curiosity, care, confidence in these conversations?

◆ How can you create moments in the day that enable multiturn, thoughtful conversations?

◆ How can you bring more curiosity and care to your conversations with children? How might you instill confidence during and through those conversations?

9

Manager and modeler of risk-taking

We are in a profession often referred to as "early childhood care *and* education." A vital part of learning, or education, is having opportunities to experience intellectual, physical, and social-emotional risk. As we've discussed previously, one of the roles of the educator is also to ensure children are *cared* for by providing a safe space for such learning. In other words, children need opportunities for risky experiences in a space that is nurturing and responsive during those experiences.

What is risk, and why is it important? For us, risk is about being vulnerable. This means you're exposed to the possibility of being physically or emotionally hurt. To most, this sounds quite awful because it's uncomfortable—for both those experiencing the vulnerability and those around them. Yet, Brené Brown (2010), a social scientist who studies vulnerability, says, "Vulnerability is the birthplace of innovation, creativity, and change." In other words, wonderful things can happen when we allow ourselves to be vulnerable. Childhood should be a place of innovation, creativity, and change. After all, children, as they develop and grow, are inherently ever-changing. They are learning to be creative in their thinking, personally innovate by learning ways of being in the world, and so forth.

Given that risk is about being vulnerable, we do not limit risk to just physical risk, which seems to be common in education.

DOI: 10.4324/9781003374053-9

We believe that children need physical risk, yes, but they also need intellectual and social-emotional risk. Thus, we explore all three (i.e., intellectual, social-emotional, and physical) aspects of risk. We see the adult playing three important roles related to risk: (1) being a model of risk-taking themselves, (2) providing opportunities for risky experiences, and (3) managing the risks in those experiences.

The following terms are connected with risk-taking:

Challenge—a task or situation that tests someone's abilities
Vulnerability—the quality or state of being exposed to the possibility of being attacked or harmed, either physically or emotionally
Hazard—a potential source of danger
Risk—a situation involving exposure to danger
Fear—an unpleasant emotion caused by the belief that someone or something is dangerous, likely to cause pain, or a threat

---

Modeling risk-taking

As we've already mentioned, we believe the educator must be aware of and adjust their own thinking and behavior when interacting with children. The way this plays out in terms of risk is being a risk-taker oneself. In other words, educators must model taking risks to show children that it's OK to be vulnerable. This vulnerability is why the characteristic of humility is so important for educators to possess.

Intellectual risk
In terms of intellectual risk, adults can model risk-taking by going public with ideas or theories in what we might call "first-draft thinking." This means you make yourself vulnerable to the possibility of not being "right" or being challenged by someone else. But by going public with ideas, you model intellectual risk-taking—that we're all constantly revising our thinking by making ourselves vulnerable and learning from others.

Social-emotional risk

Like intellectual risk, modeling social-emotional risk-taking involves being vulnerable with our interactions with others or experiencing and sharing various emotions. This, for example, might mean embracing and working through your own fear of heights by standing on a tall rock or your own fear of snakes by touching with one finger a snake someone else is holding. For some educators, it's a social-emotional risk to act silly in front of co-workers or parents. For others, it might mean working with a new co-teacher.

Physical risk

Physical risk is the most talked-about type of risk in children's play, but it isn't always discussed in terms of educators' risk-taking themselves. This is primarily due to the fact that most physical risks in early years settings are designed for the physical development of young children, but there are still moments for modeling physical risk-taking. There may be opportunities, for example, to balance on a wobbly log. Do you have a slackline in the outdoor play area for children to balance on? When was the last time *you* tried balancing on it?

Providing opportunities for risky experiences

The second important role educators play regarding modeling and facilitating risk-taking is providing opportunities for risky experiences. In other words, opportunities for intellectual, social-emotional, and physical challenges—opportunities to grow and stretch. It's important, by the way, to note the opportunities we said *opportunities*. We did not say forced experiences. An important part of providing risky experiences is allowing children to choose how and when they engage with those experiences. Yes, you may acknowledge the discomfort and then encourage children to push through, but they have the right to refuse that challenge. This means it may take a child days, weeks, or even months to engage in a particular intellectual, social-emotional, or physical risk—and that is perfectly acceptable!

Opportunities for intellectual risk

Providing opportunities for experiences related to intellectual risk means moments where children can share their ideas and theories or challenge themselves to go beyond their current thinking on a topic. This might mean asking a child to explain their theory about why or how a particular scientific phenomenon occurred. You might, for example, ask them, "Why do you think the spider made its web in that shape?" You're asking them to make their thinking public, which makes them vulnerable to the group. Another example might be asking them to count higher than they've ever counted before. Asking a child to read aloud may be an intellectual risk. For many adults, reading aloud to a group is not only an intellectual risk but also an emotional one in that it triggers anxiety. It's for this reason that it's important to keep in mind we have separated the risk into three distinct categories—intellectual, physical, social-emotional—but any sort of risk is likely to bring an emotional response as well. For us, this once again highlights how we need to constantly be considering the whole child—not just one aspect of their development.

Opportunities for social-emotional risk

Experiences related to social-emotional risk mean moments in which children feel discomfort about interacting with other people or their own emotions around any other intellectual or physical challenge. Essentially, experiences provide children with opportunities to stretch themselves in terms of their social and emotional development.

You may be asking, "How do I provide such experiences?" Well, the reality is these experiences come in a myriad of forms throughout the day and will vary from child to child in terms of what feels "risky" to them. For some children, changing the location of your group meeting can feel risky. (You may be thinking this will feel impossible for some of your children. We'll address this later when we discuss managing experiences.)

Another experience might include asking children to stand or speak in front of the whole group, such as at morning meeting, to hear their name and be recognized as part of the class. Yet another experience might be asking a classmate, teacher, or family volunteer for help in building a structure out of blocks. Yet another social-emotional risk might be meeting new people, which could include meeting children from a different classroom within the school, interacting with a guest presenter, or meeting parents or grandparents of classmates.

Opportunities for physical risk

Experiences related to physical risk mean moments during which children could become physically injured. Ironically, this is the type of risk most often discussed, and yet, of the three risks we've discussed, it is the easiest injury from which children can recover. Despite the possibility of injury, children's bodies need the opportunity to move and grow. Opportunities for physical risk allow children to move their bodies to develop physical strength and stamina. This supports not only their physical health but also their ability to engage with other learning. For example, when young children have the physical core strength to sit upright without fidgeting, they're better able to attend to cognitive tasks (Hanscom, 2016).

Opportunities for physical development through risk come in many different forms. Researcher Ellen Sandseter of Norway has described six types of risky play that are particularly connected to physical risk:

1. Great heights
2. High speed
3. Dangerous tools
4. Dangerous elements
5. Rough-and-tumble play
6. Disappearing or getting lost

Early childhood educators should strive to offer all these types of risky play in as many physical locations as possible. What is "possible" will be explored more fully when we consider how to manage risky experiences. The point here being that children need a wide variety of opportunities for physical risk through play.

Managing risky experiences

Ultimately, our goal with risky experiences is to teach children the skills to prevent emotional and physical injury for themselves. Of course, this doesn't begin immediately. Like all learning, we scaffold this process for them. We do this by helping mitigate, or manage, the risk. First, we remove hazards for children. That is, we remove the things likely to harm children and over which they would not expect or have no control. Second, we verbalize and make explicit our risk management process. Finally, but perhaps most importantly, we have conversations with children about the possibilities of harm and how we could reduce the chances of harm. These three aspects manifest differently in intellectual and social-emotional risk situations versus physical risk situations. We explore these in more detail in the following sections.

Managing intellectual and social-emotional risk

When managing intellectual and social-emotional risks, we first remove potential hazards—that is, things likely to harm them. Sometimes identifying these hazards can be a challenge. This is where knowing your individual children is vital. What are their life experiences, fears, and skills that might impact their ability to cope with the stress of various risky situations. We mentioned earlier, for example, that one way to provide social-emotional risk might be to change the location of your group meeting. As you likely know, for some children, this can feel impossible, and they will not be able to cope. For those children, we, of course, build in supports to make the experience feel less risky—visual reminders of the new schedule and location, for example.

Once we've removed the hazards for children, our management is about helping children navigate the world of risk. When it comes to intellectual and social-emotional risk the biggest way, we help children navigate risk is to create a community culture that is supportive and caring—thus safe for intellectual and social-emotional risk-taking. Keep in mind, a culture might feel safe for physical risk, but intellectual and social-emotional risk may feel altogether different. This is where we return to the personal characteristics of "inclusivity" by ensuring children feel a sense of belonging in the group. Do children feel their individual experiences and contributions are valued within the community? Furthermore, is the community culture one which embraces making mistakes. This is where the characteristic of humility comes into play for both teachers and children. Do community members embrace the fact they are imperfect humans, or is the culture one that shames individuals for their imperfections? The goal of course is to shift to a culture where all individuals are valued—imperfections and all.

Managing physical risk

Just as with intellectual and social-emotional risk, when it comes to physical risk, we begin by removing hazards. This means removing things likely to cause harm or that children cannot control for themselves. This is the basis of health regulations— eliminating those things most likely to harm children. This includes, for example, a maximum temperature for hot water for handwashing sinks. In the outdoor play area, this would include things like removing overhanging dead branches or hazardous plants such as poison ivy.

Once the hazards are removed, the next step is to conduct a dynamic risk assessment with children. Based on the work by Tim Gill, an author who specializes in risky play for children, this process involves engaging the children in a conversation around the following three questions:

1. What is great about doing this activity? (benefits)
2. How might we (or nature) get hurt doing this activity? (hazards)
3. How can we keep ourselves, each other, and nature safe doing this activity? (procedures)

The first question highlights the benefits of the activity; the second, hazards that may or may not be clearly evident to children; and the third, the procedures. Conversations around these questions can occur any time a new activity is about to commence.

The conversations can also be documented in writing to capture the community's thinking around certain activities.

Supporting children to assess risky experiences for themselves

Once we have created a safe, caring culture we can then help children to verbalize their feelings around risk. Doing so means helping children identify, label, and respond to their emotions around risk in intellectual, social-emotional, and physical situations. This not only supports their executive function skills, but it also provides them with control over their own lives and furthers their ability to identify, label, and respond to emotions, leading to children becoming assessors of their own risky experiences. You know you've been successful in creating strong assessors when children say things like, "I'm a little scared, but nothing can hurt me too badly so I think I'll try it," or "I'm feeling really nervous but I think I can do it," or "I can remember how to get up on the branch, I looked and it looks strong, what do you think?"

The formal process for managing risk as we've described earlier is critical to developing children who are independent assessors of risk. Another critical element is modeling for children our own risk assessment with explicit language and narration. This can be in our own risk-taking as discussed at the opening of the chapter or when observing children. The following suggestions use positive language that encourages the child to be a participant in the process.

WHAT IT SOUNDS LIKE: EXAMPLES OF LANGUAGE RELATED TO RISK MANAGEMENT

Children are either involved in risk management or they are not. The more they are involved, the more they will come to understand and therefore keep themselves safe in all aspects of their education. Here are some examples of language we might use here when being intentional about risk management with children:

Internal language or language with co-teachers

"Anthony is finding playing outside in the snow really physically and emotionally challenging. He may need just a bit more comfort. Let's talk with the family about how we can all help him understand how to keep warm. Woolen socks are number one."

"How could we help those two to play together consistently and avoid unfriendly words?"

"The area by the fallen log has become really slippery after all the rain. Who would like to work with the children on making hazard signs?"

"I'm starting to think I'm not much of a risk-taker. I'd appreciate your encouragement when I seem hesitant to try something new."

Language to use with children

Adults modeling risk-taking

"I'm not sure, but I'm wondering if that bird is a pileated woodpecker." *(intellectual risk)*

"Hmm, this is just a guess, but I wonder if that word is pronounced …" *(intellectual risk)*

"I'm really nervous around snakes, but I'm going to try touching it with one finger." *(physical and social-emotional risk)*

"I find it hard to meet new people, but I'm going to introduce myself to our guest." *(social-emotional risk)*

"I'm not sure about balancing on this log, but I'll give it a try." *(physical risk)*

Supporting risk-taking

"You seem nervous about this activity. How could I help you feel more comfortable?"

"What is your plan?"

"Talk me through what's good about doing this? What is a bit tricky? How can we make it less tricky?"

Whilst looking back at the documentation on risk: "Do you see here in our Floorbook we talked about what we were going to do to make the fire area less risky? It was hard work, but we agreed that only the Fire Marshall [one designated child] can feed the fire. That didn't happen today; why?"

"Your face is making me think you're nervous about balancing on this log. You can try it now or wait until another time if you prefer."

Self-reflection

♦ This week observe how often you take risks yourself during the school day:
  ♦ Do you talk about your own risk-taking with children?
  ♦ How does that feel when you do?
♦ How often do you and your team conduct benefit–risk assessments?
♦ How often do you revisit policies and procedures you've established for higher risk activities within your program?
♦ Think about the ways you talk with children about risk-taking:
  ♦ How are children involved? Do you engage in conversation or tell them the procedures to follow?
  ♦ How often do you use the benefit–risk assessment procedure with children?
  ♦ How do you involve children to be risk managers across the curriculum? Do you use picture sequences to support children in remembering safety procedures?
  ♦ Do you share with them how you're feeling about a particular situation and what you're going to do about it?

10

Provocateur

What do we mean by "provocation"?

There is a tension in the world of play as people struggle with the understanding of what it is and how we support it, if in fact we should at all. A way to view play in relation to this book has been framed around the idea of the influence we have over the space, time, and resources we provide and nestled in the middle of all that is our role as adults. This is the S.T.A.R. that guides us in our work (Warden, 2007) and through adjusting these things we undoubtedly influence children's experiences. We can use the same resources to respond, provocate, invite, or instruct.

In relation to this, we have different ways we can offer an experience. Table 10.1 provides a simplified example that shows four levels ofthe increasing structure and expectation adults introduce to the learning environment.

A provocation is defined by its open-ended nature, it can be a resource, an encounter, or an interaction as we explore later in this chapter. Children choose if, how, and when they engage with it. It is designed to stimulate curiosity and challenge thinking as it is usually connected to an observation made by an adult of children's fascinations. For some children, it initiates, deepens, or seeks to engage them in something they may not be aware of. The Scottish curriculum framework titled *Realising the Ambition* (2020) states that "we have a key role to play in providing motivating learning provocations and appropriate

DOI: 10.4324/9781003374053-10

TABLE 10.1 Four examples of adult intent

Self-discovered	Provocation (open-ended)	Invitation (expectation to engage)	Instruction (adult directed)
A snail shell found in the garden by Lara	Display of snail shells: reference book about snails; images of cartoon and real snails; story linked to snail; 3D model of a snail	Adult selects the resource to use to share with children	Materials about snails are not displayed but available
Adult notices: "Wow that is interesting, what a discovery!"	Adult draws attention to display if required and records ideas through observation: "What do you think of snails?"	Adult has planned experiences: "We are studying snails, who would like to make a model in clay?"	Adult: "Come to the carpet area, we are going to hear about Laras snail and read a story."

challenges". Our richer knowledge of the world helps young children to make progress in their learning. The adult and child learning to construct learning is described as shared sustained thinking, in these moments children and practitioners work together to take learning further than the child could by themselves (Siraj-Blatchford 2009).

An invitation is used to ask children to engage with a specific concept, skill, or piece of knowledge. Technically, an invitation can be refused, but in our experiences, the language that is used not only invites engagement, but there is often also an implicit message that the adult wants the children to complete a task. Unlike a provocation, there is a more intentional structure provided by the adult to frame the learning. This role was found to be a key to quality and progression in the Effective Provision in Pre-School Education project (Sylva et al., 2004).

A defined action that is done purposely to facilitate learning (Reigeluth and Carr-Chellman, 2009) is instructional. The instructional teaching is key here as the adult creates a deliberate series of experiences that they believe will enhance learning.

In nature-based pedagogy, we teach the name of a plant or animal, how to light a fire, or how to tie a knot, these are instructional. In terms of monitoring the breadth and balance of curricular experiences and, indeed, progression, there are times when this is the appropriate strategy for inclusion within playful inquiries that are centered around co-constructivism to ensure that everyone has equality of access.

Always being aware of the potential and possibilities of play

In the first example of self-discovery, there is high child autonomy, and within provocations, there is a huge amount of potential. Possibility planning is a phrase used by Warden (2020) to describe the style of planning where the adults consider the possibilities that may arise during encounters with the natural world or materials from it, linked to experiences that children have created themselves before. The visual mind maps, as shown in Figure 10.1, are therefore collated from previous children's experiences and used to provoke a subsequent group to share what they want to do. This is more child-centered than an adult creating one on their own. The mind map has images and drawings to support children to understand what is written.

The adult can put the visual mind map in the Floorbook as evidence of the provocation. Children can return to it and add more lines of inquiry and things they want to do at any point.

The pedagogical dance of child-initiated and teacher-led

The adult and child enter a dance in co-constructing the inquiry or emergent curriculum (Warden, 2015). Partnering children in this way means that we need to understand the steps as each day

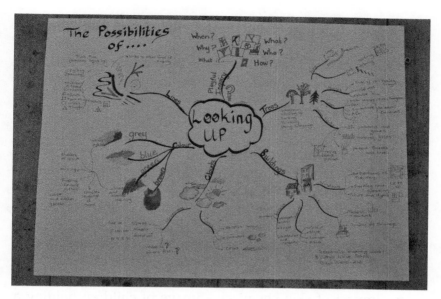

FIGURE 10.1 Visual mind map.

we change the pace, move in a new direction, select new partners in learning, and bring an inquiry to a close.

Supporting curiosity, confidence, and care

Using provocations, invitations, and instructions are only three possible ways that we change the level of support for children. It is our opinion that in an environment where there is a respectful, kind, and open balance between adults and children, children feel more at ease to ask questions and show their curiosity; they feel more relaxed to embrace failure and develop a growth mindset that leads to confidence and ultimately trust the adults around them to be vulnerable emotionally and display care of themselves, others, and the natural world. Let us look at three types of provocation to demonstrate the difference the adult role could make in relation to these three aspects.

Provocation through resources (i.e., living and nonliving)

Displays of material related to snails that we detailed earlier in Table 10.1 could be extended to share a number of additional provocations:

Curiosity
◆ Closer study (e.g., magnifiers)
◆ Understanding of movement (e.g., glass/Perspex to look at the underneath)
◆ Variety within species (e.g., ID chart of the variety and complexity of snails)
◆ Relevance (e.g., Local species found in their garden)

Care
◆ Impact of skin chemicals—image of children holding a leaf with a snail on it
◆ Human responsibility—menu of snail food, water spray
◆ Needs—terrarium with wood, soil, vegetation
◆ Rights of nature—countdown of days until release

Confidence
◆ Observing—image of child looking closely at snail
◆ Identity—cultural representation in images
◆ Voices—children's theories and ideas written up and on display
◆ Value–QR code with a film or audio of children explaining what they know/have found out about snails

Provocation through experience (e.g., storytelling, farmer visit)

Knowledge is held in people as well as books and digital platforms. Involving children in arranging the visit may take more time but increases the authenticity and engagement. Inviting children to question and engage with real people teaches them that we all have different perspectives and if we show we are curious and caring they will appreciate it. Increasing the diversity and frequency of meeting people outside the family unit has become a valid strategy since the COVID-19 pandemic to increase social confidence.

Curiosity
♦ Diversity of opinion—giving children access to the local community through excursions and incursions
♦ Expertise—using introductions to make it visible: "This is Rachel. She has worked with birds for 10 years and has learned a lot."
♦ Empowerment—"We have found a lot about cows, but we had a few tricky questions that we wrote down so that we wouldn't forget. Let me read them from the Floorbook."

Care
♦ Comfort—"How can we make Tony feel comfortable? What might he like?"
♦ Care—"Where should we be? Are we standing or sitting? It is important that we all feel OK."
♦ Gratitude—whole adult team demonstrates thanks and care on arrival, sending thanks after a visit with children.

Confidence
♦ Support—"Chris, we were talking the other day and you wanted to know how corn knows when to stop growing. They were interesting ideas; you could ask that now."
♦ Agency—"Let us write a letter asking them to come."
♦ Consultation—"What was your favorite moment? What shall we do next?"
♦ Modeling—"It can make me nervous when I meet new people. Here is a photo of the person we are meeting next week, so we know who is coming to visit."

Provocation of interaction

Considering yourself as a provocation stems from the idea that you, like any other human, have a story to share full of concepts, skills, and knowledge. When we are away from buildings, the idea of a display becomes a log to collect finds, a book may become a story to tell, magnifiers are in the children's rucksacks, and discoveries are made as you travel through space or at a base camp. In this dynamic space, our interactions, stepping in and out of the conversations, are very fluid, and the words we use and all the aspects of tone position we discussed in Chapter 7 become even more vital. Some models of nature immersion such as Waldkindergartens in Germany (Warden, 2012a) and Bush Kinder in Australia (Warden and Fargher, 2023) are built around stepping back to provide more agency to children. In this model, the adult is a resource that can be accessed if needed. The exchange of the possibilities is through conversations on the journey to the site or at a gathering time and the environment is viewed as the ultimate provider of provocations:

Curiosity
◆ Anticipation—"I wonder what we will find today?"
◆ Recall—"Last week you found that log shaped like a duck head; perhaps it is still there."
◆ Reminder—"The puddle was really deep last time, perhaps use the puddle measurer before you go in unless you have spare boots with you."

Care
◆ Gratitude—"What shall we say thanks for before we go into the forest?"
◆ Modeling—leave nothing but footprints
◆ Appreciation—"Feel, look, listen and smell—what a wonderful place to be."
◆ For resources—"We only take a few sticks because the other things here like bugs, need them too."
◆ Community—model care for each other staff and children: "You look unhappy. How can you help yourself feel more comfortable?"

Confidence

◆ Speaking out—being alongside the child and observing other languages they use

◆ Social engagement—"Perhaps you could ask? What words could you use?"

◆ Failure—"The joy of being out here is it is full of medals of adventure—falling off the tree stump may leave a bruise, but then you can tell the story of how you got that medal!"

In summary, embracing the concept and style of provocation allows the adult to adopt a more consultative role, with respectful encounters that value both children's and adults' ideas.

WHAT IT SOUNDS LIKE: EXAMPLES OF LANGUAGE RELATED TO USING PROVOCATIONS IN PRACTICE

Understanding the difference in adult intent between a provocation, invitation, or instruction supports us to be aware of the words and phrases we use with children and the impact that they have. Here are some examples of the language we use when working in an environment that uses provocations and possibilities.

Internal language or language with co-teachers:

"What interest was there in the leaf and magnifiers put out today?"

"Do you think that we should talk about the new blocks or offer a provocation that invites them to investigate themselves?"

"I have some interesting images of a flies' eyes following Andrew's fascination with the dead fly he found. His theory was that it couldn't see and bumped into the window. I am going to share them at small-group time and see what happens."

"What do you think the connection could be between their fascination with snail shells, strangler vines, and the rope they took apart yesterday? I am wondering if it could be twisting or spiraling?"

Language to use with children:

"I was wondering if you could show me how to do that" (Child leads)

"Perhaps I could show you how I think that could work?" (Adult leads)

"What objects should we put into our Talking Tub to talk about at our meeting? Let us think about things to do with spirals- I had a lollipop that was shaped in a spiral, I might look for a picture of that."

"Now it is time to do this xxxx; then we can do what you asked. Let me write it down so we don't forget to do it." (Adult negotiation)

"Thank you for bringing that in. Can you share with us what you know or want to find out. It makes me think of a lot of questions."

Self-reflection

- ◆ Consider your past week:
  - ◆ How much of the learning was around a provocation?
  - ◆ Were there points where you used an instruction? Or a clear invitation?
  - ◆ What phrases do you use when children refuse to engage?
  - ◆ How much did you use operational language around routines rather than thinking?
- ◆ How much challenge and progression do you offer in your planning?
- ◆ When you look over previous planning sheets, do you make it clear how you will engage children in the experiences through displays? Setup?

11

Mentor, guide, and leader

As young children, we were both constantly outdoors with the older children. They perceived their role to be our mentors, put us in tricky situations, and let us get out of them. They were guides when they gave us tips to avoid stinging nettles, and finally, they were often power-hungry leaders who made us feel that we were at the bottom of the pecking order. This sort of mentorship and guidance are not new concepts, as many First Nation peoples have embraced the sense of walking alongside as a way of supporting learning. These voices are authentically and respectfully shared through an edited book by Warden and Fargher (2023) titled *Beyond the Gate*. The diverse Indigenous voices demonstrate deep care around the balance of the needs of children, culture, and the natural world.

Apprenticeship approach

In our childhood scenario mentioned earlier, there was a sense of being an apprentice, someone who was learning from those more skilled than us. It is interesting that in our conversations, we have a common experience from two different countries about how, to use my mother's phrase, we had "the sharp edges knocked off us" in that we learned to be more humble and embrace advice given to us in many different ways. The complexity of our roles now is undoubtedly affected by the way adults and older children

DOI: 10.4324/9781003374053-11

treated us when we were young. Understanding this storied childhood and its impact on us as professionals is fundamental to considering how we will be at different points with children now we are adults. We are aware that we seek to support curiosity, confidence, and care, but how do we do that by adopting the roles of mentor, guide, and leader? Let us look at how we can explore concepts, skills, and knowledge in, about, and with the natural world as they are abundant when we embrace nature pedagogy.

The importance of concepts, skills, and knowledge

There are many aspects to learning. The literature often groups the vastness of knowing into three aspects: concepts, skills, and knowledge. In this work we see a concept as being an intangible, main idea that helps us understand big ideas such as growth or movement. A skill is a practical, active thing that we do that helps us understand theoretical ideas (e.g., skipping, walking), whereas knowledge is information that a society deems to be the truth.

Our role as adults is suggested by White (2002) as being able to explain, give examples, and monitor children's understanding, because in his view, children will not just pick concepts up. This is linked to Vygotsky (1986) and his suggestion that there are formal and scientific concepts and that although both connect through home-based and school-based experiences, the role of the adult is key as they engage in a zone of development, offering links and connections to other existing concepts. When we explored as children, we experienced spirality, revisiting a concept, and using language to support a shared understanding that is mediated by what each person thinks—the adult and the child.

There are many roles and strategies outlined in this book, Willig (1990) suggests five strategies that adults should consider when they are working with children with a lens on learning:

◆ Matching teaching material to the ability of the learner
◆ Disturbing the learner's existing ideas
◆ Teaching by telling
◆ Learning from observing
◆ Learning by thinking about thinking

The third point would appear to be problematic for co-constructivist thinking as Duckworth (1987) asserts, "Simply telling children the truth about something could not make them understand it" (p. 32). However, as we have explored in this chapter as a leader, there are points where knowledge is told. We can go to books and reference materials outside, the internet, and people in the community who may have knowledge that we can learn from. The key here is balance as in all elements so the roles of mentor, guide, and leader can be used to great effect to adjust the pacing and content of our planning. Hannust and Kikas (2010) and Driver (1983) reminded us that when over-loaded or confused by information, children often revert back to earlier intuitions. So, repetition of experience is important so that with each encounter the child develops a new slightly adjusted thought. Paley (1981) refers to this as "concepts that are held in temporary custody," a phrase that captures the fleeting nature of the learning encounters we have with children whether we are Inside, Outside, or Beyond.

The holistic nature of learning with nature bends itself to the scientific realm. Nunes (1995) urges us to be aware as adults of the '"ways of thinking" (p. 194) rather than the accumulation of facts about the natural world. This supports Valanides et al. (2000) as they suggest careful observation and exploration of children's current understanding need to be the starting points for plan-ning. We explored this in Chapters 5 and 6 when we explored effective planning and documentation.

A guide walks alongside a child, listening and disrupting some ideas through subtle interactions. There is a balance and respect of what it means to know, that truth is subjective and ideas that children hold are their truths and as such are as valid as those cre-ated by the greatest minds. Wadsworth (1997) is noted by Robson (2006, p. 166) as suggesting that awareness of the different kinds of ideas children hold will be important for adults in supporting children. They note some concepts and ideas from their practice in science that are interesting to consider; they are noted here with some language and behaviors used by children in our practice:

◆ Anthropomorphic views: "Don't be sad tree, that your leaves have fallen off."

- ◆ Egocentric views: "The flowers are looking at me, because I smile a lot."
- ◆ Ideas around the use of colloquial use of language: "Wee stones float—that's what my mum said."
- ◆ Ideas based on limited experience and observations: "That's the wind knocking to come in."
- ◆ Stylized representations: children draw the sun with lines around it; water is drawn as blue and grass as green.

Preparing ourselves as adults to be aware of some of the possibilities for children's awareness of the natural world is fundamental to being a nature pedagogue.

Helping children apply skills and core knowledge to practical situations

The balance of an awareness of concepts, the application of skills, and the growth of knowledge is fundamental to the approach you adopt when you teach. If we view language as a way to make sense of learning, as detailed earlier, then it becomes core to the purpose of our interactions. The question is does the natural world and our role in children's care and education have any impact on language and therefore learning. There is extensive research that supports the place of nature-based experiences and children's social and cognitive development. In a time of technological development, there is more research emerging that questions the place of technology and what Richard Louv (2005) refers to as secondhand learning. In a study that looked at a link between language use and a nature-based environment, Cameron-Faulkner et al. (2017) showed that the direct experience of nature (being in a botanical garden) compared to indirect experience (photos and books of nature elements), resulted in a wider range of nature words during parent–child talk. As advocates of nature-based work, physically being with nature is central but perhaps in the right way digital representations can improve accessibility.

Four themes were identified around the acquisition of language skills in nature-based environments in a study by Prins et al. (2023):

- ◆ Children used language to refer to their play situation.
- ◆ Children used language to refer to the elements of their physical play environment.
- ◆ Compared to the non-nature-based playground, children talked more about the objects of the nature-based playground.
- ◆ Children talked more about science and math concepts.

Play in the nature-based playground appeared to be a richer conversational setting for language use than the non-nature-based playground, with a potential to scaffold and guide language use. There are always limitations to research and one could argue that no mention was made of the other curricular areas beyond science and math; however, what we can take from this is that the play affordance and flexibility of a nature based environment offers us an opportunity to "scaffold and guide language" (Prins et al., 2023, p. 1).

Mentoring as a bridge—from here to there and now to then

In the writing around documentation, we talked about it being used as a method of holding memories. There are many ways that we interact as mentors that can bring those memories alive or indeed navigate situations by building bridges for the child. These bridges may be from where the child stands on the periphery of the play looking on to where they appear to want to be. Getting down low and looking alongside the child allows the adult to adopt a mentoring role. In that one moment there may be the following:

- ◆ **Silent affirmation**: "We are both here."
- ◆ **A retrospective question**: "I am wondering what they are doing?"

- **A question**: "Andrew, what can you see? What do you think they are doing?"
- **Descriptive language**: "I can see John is digging with the spade in the sand pit. Lara is next to him building a tower."
- **Suggestion**: "I wonder what we could do if we went over there?"
- **Provocation**: "Diggers can make bigger holes than a spade—how big could we make a hole?"
- **Invitation**: "There is space by Jo; shall we go over there and see what we can make with the digger?"
- **Instruction**: "In 3 minutes, we are going to go over there to get ready for lunch. Here is the egg timer so we can watch the time pass."
- **Transfer of knowledge**: "That yellow digger is a JCB."

The list could go on and demonstrates all the nuances and complexities we have in our use of language. Each phrase changes the experience and the message the child receives, therefore affecting the development of curiosity, confidence, and care.

We can build bridges between what children know and what they are experiencing. In earlier chapters, we explored our role in planning and documentation; these are formalized ways of recording. Our skills as mentors and guides are used all the time to help children make connections across their lived experiences to deepen learning that can then be recorded if required. Let us look at the moment when a 3-year-old child picks up a daffodil in the garden and stands looking at it. Ideally there would be a slow conversation or indeed just an observation, but for the purpose of this book, let us consider our options to help the child recall and connect her experiences. In that one moment, there may be the following:

- **Information**: "You have a yellow daffodil."
- **Affirmation of a choice**: "It was a good choice to pick that up off the ground; the bees need the other flowers to stay alive so they can get some food."

- ◆ **Modeling care**: "Shall we get a vase for that to keep it alive a little longer?"
- ◆ **Memory recall**: "I remember when we picked daffodils to take home to your family."
- ◆ **Links to home**: "Your mum said that she put your flowers in a vase on the table. She said, 'Thank you for the flowers. I love them.' I remember her smiling at the door when she picked you up."
- ◆ **Links between events at the setting**: "I can see that you like flowers. The last time you had the paints out you were painting with a lot of green and different yellows and then you looked like you were enjoying looking at the flower books in the reading area."
- ◆ **Sharing possibilities**: "What do you want to do with the flower? I know where there is a vase. Or maybe you could make it into flower soup."

Research into the relationship of adult understanding of theory and practice is explored extensively in recent research from the Nordic countries by Waltzer, Kärkkäinen, and Nuutinen (2023). In this work, they explore how adults perceive their role and how they are trained to use pedagogy in practice.

The training and qualifications required for working in early childhood education (ECE) vary across the world. Societies differ in terms of how they set expectations concerning ECE as well as the kinds of theoretical frameworks that ECE is built on (Barnett et al., 2009; Broström, 2017).

Scotland is moving toward a degree-led profession. All managers (heads of center) have to hold a degree in education to take up the role. These additional qualifications have been fully funded by the Scottish government to really drive the added value of increasing the professional use of child development to understand how children learn. The United States has a similar approach.

A child-centered orientation and knowledge of individual child development are not sufficient, as theoretical knowledge regarding teaching and learning is also required to formulate good-quality pedagogy in relation to ECE (Agbenyega, 2012; Broström, 2017).

It is perhaps significant that not all ECE training includes specific details around possible approaches to interaction and from experience some adults have a natural aptitude to connect to and understand children. Colleagues we have met and elders in our profession did not all hold qualifications; instead, they slowed enough to seek out the child and came to know them. This intuition is challenging to teach as it requires empathy and an authentic interest in what children have to say, do, and make. They were interesting, warm, and caring human beings.

In reality, none of us (qualified or not) know the real impact of what we do or say with children. In 2012, Dooley and Fitzpatrick, at University College Dublin, published a study about children and young people's mental health and well-being. A key finding was the importance of a kind and reliable relationship with "one good adult" to buffer against difficulties, offer support, and believe in the child or young person. Children and young people described teachers, sports coaches, and parents as examples of "good adults" who made a real difference to their mental health and well-being. The concept of one good adult has captured the importance of safe, supportive relationships for children and young people's mental health and well-being. In collaboration with children, a job description was created to give to adults who want to work in care and education.

THIS IS THE ONE GOOD ADULT JOB DESCRIPTION:

The children and young people of Scotland want to recruit "good adults" to work with them and alongside them in a range of settings.

Essential Criteria
◆ You must be authentic, calm, approachable, and welcoming.
◆ You encourage and help young people to find support if they need it.

◆ You must be kind! Respect and try to understand children and young people and their lived experience. Take their concerns and worries seriously.

◆ You must ask clear questions, actively listen to children and young people's answers, and explain any actions you will take.

◆ You demonstrate that you're worthy of trust by doing what you say you will

◆ You are open-minded and fair. You don't jump to conclusions or judge.

◆ You recognise that all children and young people are individuals. The person in front of you will need a personalized approach and supports.

◆ You trust that the child or young person in front of you knows themself. You ask for and listen to their views, and you don't patronize them.

◆ You treat children and young people as your equal and talk directly to them.

◆ You offer realistic, helpful advice.

Desirable Criteria

◆ You are hopeful about the individual you are talking to, as well as the support you can offer them.

◆ You encourage children and young people to embrace their strengths. You are enthusiastic and positive about what they can do.

◆ You notice when children and young people are struggling and know the next steps to take to help them.

◆ You know when to use humor, and when to be serious.

◆ You help young people relax by being friendly, caring and putting them at ease.

Skills and experience

◆ You welcome children and young people from all different backgrounds and experiences.

◆ You understand that all children and young people have mental health, just like everyone has physical health, and sometimes they need support with this.

◆ You understand that we all have emotions, thoughts and behaviors that affect our mental health, and that is perfectly normal.

◆ You recognise that individuals aren't defined by just one aspect of their life or experiences.

◆ You want to learn about issues that affect children and young people's lives (including their experiences of gender, sexuality, disability, race, and care). You consider the ways these experiences might impact wellbeing and mental health.

◆ You understand the difference that positive relationships can make.

◆ You want to be a trusted, reliable adult for children and young people, no matter what your job is.

(2012, p. 4)

It is humbling to read what children say they want as it suggests they may not have encountered adults like this. Although it is written through a lens of supporting children with mental illnesses, it can be applied to any adult and provides a stimulus for all of us to consider what our interview would be like with children asking the questions. In conversation with children at Auchlone Nature Kindergarten with a new prospective candidate, they are asked: "What are your hugs like? Can you smile?" That perhaps says it all.

WHAT IT SOUNDS LIKE: EXAMPLES OF LANGUAGE RELATED TO BEING A MENTOR, GUIDE, AND LEADER

In our lived experience, a mentor is someone who is an experienced and trusted advisor who encourages people to find their own solutions, a guide is someone who shows others the way, and a leader is someone who takes the lead. So given this, there is a shift in the level of autonomy and direction provided. Here are some examples of language we might use when being a mentor, a guide, or a leader.

Internal language or language with co-teachers

"How could we improve the engagement in the sand area?" (mentor)

"Here are some suggestions and possibilities for sand play for us to look at and choose some provocations to use." (guide)

"Introducing different levels into the sand area will improve their engagement; when will we start to try that?" (leader)

"I wonder what job description our children would write for us?"

Language to use with children

"I wonder how you could fix those sticks together?" (mentor)

"There are ropes, wire, and wool over there; perhaps they would help you fix the sticks together." (guide)

"Let me show you a lashing and a knot that will help you fix those two sticks together." (leader)

"What kind of person do you enjoy being with?"

Self-reflection

◆ Take time to consider over one day how you move between the three different styles of interaction:
  ◆ What impact was there on the children?
  ◆ Which style of interaction evoked more engagement from the children?
  ◆ Which role made you feel more comfortable? why?
◆ Listen to your colleagues and reflect on the roles that they adopt. How do they support curiosity? Care? Confidence?
◆ Consider the mentors, guides, and leaders in your professional life. How did their approaches make you feel? What can this teach you about how to be with children?

12

Advocate

The last role of early childhood educators we explore is far from the least important. However, it may be one of the most complex. That is the role of an advocate. Educators advocate for young children in a myriad of ways—both inside and outside of the classroom. To be an advocate means to support or defend a group or a cause. In this case, we're suggesting that educators defend children as a whole and their right to have safe, happy, healthy, and flourishing childhoods.

Just like adults, young children have wants and needs. They have thoughts and ideas. Yet all too often, young children are marginalized and pushed aside as though they don't have voices or those voices are less valuable than adults. We are suggesting that in fact children do have voices and our role as educators is to not only listen to those voices but also amplify them. In doing so, we move closer to living the tenets described in the United Nation's Convention on the Rights of the Child (1989). It's important to also remember that the Convention on the Rights of the Child should include all children globally—no matter where they live, how they identify, or what their abilities are.

In raising up children's voices we support the development of curiosity, confidence, and care. For most of this book, we have focused on these concepts as they relate to individual children, which is very important. What is also important, however, is the

DOI: 10.4324/9781003374053-12

impact that has on local and global communities. By advocating from where we are in the world and with our unique perspectives, we are helping solve the global problems we introduce this book with (e.g., conflict, climate crisis).

Advocating Inside, Outside, and Beyond

That is what is possible with advocacy. The question that remains is, How do we advocate? For a moment, let's consider the Inside, Outside, and Beyond as a metaphor for advocacy instead of spaces for learning or social-emotional development. The Inside includes the many ways educators advocate for children within the classroom, including defending children's right to play, their time, the learning spaces, and so forth. This includes all the other roles we've mentioned in this book around how we structure our day; the space, time, and materials we provide; and the language we use with children. We can also advocate for individual children with other children in the classroom. For example, when one child expresses concern that other children are pulling up the flowers that the butterflies were landing on, we can ensure those thoughts are heard and discussed.

We can also advocate for all the children in our classroom as a whole. This might include advocating for the protection or addition of policies at the program or organization level. For example, perhaps your organization has a rule that children can't go outside if the temperature is below 0 °C/32 °F. In this case, you might choose to advocate for children by convincing the administration that with appropriate clothing children not only can but also should be able to play outdoors below freezing.

Outside advocacy is ensuring safe, healthy, supportive communities for young children. At this level, advocacy takes on more policy- and system-level decisions. Some of these issues will be obviously related to young children. For example, an educator might advocate for the investment in public funds to allow young children to attend quality childcare no matter their family's ability to pay. Then other Outside issues may have an impact on children in a more indirect way. Perhaps, for example, the local community is lacking parks and walking paths. Or those spaces exist, but there are challenges with drug use in those spaces. While it may not seem relevant to children, advocating to address drug use and a lack of access to green spaces directly impacts children's right to thrive in a healthy and safe community.

Advocacy from a Beyond perspective includes state/provincial, national, and global efforts to ensure children's rights. This work is heavily based in systems and the policies that establish those systems. This might include how care and education is funded, certification requirements for educators, requirements schools must meet to maintain funding, and so forth. As we have worked with educators over the years, this level of advocacy seems to be particularly daunting. This is where educators joining together can be particularly effective. A great example of this specific to nature-based pedagogy was how outdoor and nature-based educators collaborated in the state of Washington to advocate for legislation for the introduction and piloting licensing regulations for entirely outdoor preschools. Not only did that pilot project legislation pass, but the regulations are now an official part of the Washington childcare regulations. This has, in turn, led other states to begin discussions and implementation of nature-based childcare licensing regulations. So while this level of advocacy can be particularly daunting, it can also make an incredible impact.

Defenders of childhood

When considering how we can advocate, or perhaps what to advocate for, it may be helpful to think of ourselves as defenders of childhood. We as early childhood educators are on the front lines protecting, guarding, and defending children's right to a thriving childhood. Regarding children, there are many elements to consider defending:

- ◆ Expression of their home language and culture
- ◆ Right to thrive no matter their skills, abilities, or special rights
- ◆ Access to safe, rich learning spaces Inside, Outside, and Beyond (this includes advocating for the natural world!)
- ◆ Time to experience nature, to slow down, and to just be
- ◆ Healthy, ethical, and sustainable foods
- ◆ Ethically and sustainably sourced learning materials
- ◆ Right to play

This is far from an exhaustive list but, rather, a starting point for considering the many ways that we as educators can and do advocate each and every day for young children. By the way, it's also important to note that inaction or remaining silent is advocacy. The question is, Are we advocating for our desired outcomes? For example, if our program limits children's free play to 15 minutes a day and we think they should have more time, we have one of two choices. We can (1) say nothing and be complicit in the eroding of childhoods or (2) speak up and advocate for what we know is best with children. We do acknowledge that this can be challenging when your own employment and job security to care for yourself and your family may be on the line. So we're not asking you to recklessly advocate but, rather, to find the ways given your situation and power where you *can* advocate. Do what you can, where you are, with the goal of defending the childhoods of the children you care for.

As Warden said in her book *Green Teaching* (2022), "Every child on the planet has the right to play outside in the natural world, and until that goal is met, we all need to be advocates of a relationship way of working" (p. 10). The goal has not been met. We must continue to advocate.

WHAT IT SOUNDS LIKE: EXAMPLES OF LANGUAGE RELATED TO BEING AN ADVOCATE

One of our roles is to be part of a professional movement that advocates for children's rights. New rights that are becoming part of the conversation at the moment include the right to have access to the rest of the natural world and that the natural world has rights as well. It is important to note that it is not our role to force religious or political views on children through coercion but that children are encouraged to feel they can make a difference. Here are some examples of language we might use to encourage and engage in advocacy.

Internal language or language with co-teachers

"Jamal has a real sensitivity to protecting bugs. How can we help him share that passion?"

"I have shared an article in the staff area about some of the reasons we go outside. It might be interesting reading for you."

"What can I do that will make a difference tomorrow, next week, this year?"

"Did you know that we can get a grant to plant trees with the children? I did some research, and we should be eligible. Happy to organize—what do you think?"

"It's frustrating that the regulations say we can't go on a walk to the local park. Who could we talk to about that?"

Language to use with children

"I can see how you care about the bug and how angry you get when some children hurt them. How can we help them understand how cool bugs are?"

"Well done, Joseph; you put your paper into the recycling bin. The sign Ailsa made must have worked."

"Who would like to help feed the worms with today's vegetables from snack time? There may be some worms wee to feed the new tree. It's great to not throw all this good stuff in the garbage when we can use it."

Self-reflection

- ◆ Think back on the past week in the classroom:
  - ◆ In what ways did you defend children's right to play?
  - ◆ Did you provide children with time to experience a slower pace or just be?
  - ◆ What actions did you take to defend children's right to space and materials?
  - ◆ How did you support children to advocate for themselves and/or nature?
- ◆ What program or organizational policies seem counterproductive to the broader goals for supporting children? Who might you talk to about those policies?
- ◆ Reflect on your collaborations with other professionals in your community:
  - ◆ When was the last time you gathered to discuss the challenges within the early childhood profession at the community, state/provincial, or national level?
  - ◆ When was the last time you discussed challenges facing children and families?
  - ◆ Who in your community is already doing advocacy work that you might join or collaborate with?
- ◆ What organizations at the state/provincial or national level are working to advocate for young children or the natural world? How might you join in those efforts?

13

An invitation for deeper exploration

We started this book by discussing the importance of developing children's confidence, curiosity, and care. While there are many social-emotional constructs, the three categories of confidence, curiosity, and care encompass the big ideas we're striving for when we teach children. However, these three constructs are not just limited to children. We think confidence, curiosity, and care are essential for nature-based educators to be effective professionals.

We live in a world full of options and choices. Some of the hardest choices we make every day are those we choose to make in our role as an adult supporting children in care and education. Furthermore, we operate in a system that is highly regulated by ratios, rules, and routines that can leave us feeling disempowered to influence anything. Perhaps we need to hold onto the fact that it is a *choice* in those small moments of interaction between a child and an adult. While it may seem as though regulatory agencies are in control, the fact is nobody else has control over your voice, your face, your body, or your mind apart from yourself. Consider how many subtle decisions you make every day, hour, and minute that directly affect your interaction and ultimately relationship with children. For example,

DOI: 10.4324/9781003374053-13

- do you stretch your body to get down low so that you can look at each other on the same level?
- do you hold back your inner drive to *do* things for them and wait patiently as they discover and learn it for themselves?
- do you make the effort to take off your sunglasses so that they can see into your eyes?
- do you change the way you speak in a way that treats children with respect and interest?

Each of these choices is influenced by our own confidence in our abilities; how curious we are about ourselves, our co-workers, and children; and how much we care for children. Furthermore, confidence, curiosity, and care influence how we bring to life the many roles we explored in this book. We selected roles particularly relevant to working with the natural world—whether that is working inside a building, outside in an outdoor play area, or beyond the gate into wilder spaces where we discover nature on nature's terms. Having said that, who we are as positive, kind human beings influence how we treat each other and therefore the rest of the natural world.

With this in mind, this chapter is an invitation. We invite you to revisit the idea of the Inside, Outside, and Beyond as it relates to your social-emotional worlds—not just places in the class day. **We are inviting you to explore your inner world (i.e., Inside), the relationships you have with others and nature (i.e., Outside), and the connections to the unobservable (i.e., Beyond).**

CHARACTERISTICS OF THE EARLY CHILDHOOD EDUCATOR

- Self-aware
- Open to new ideas with a personal growth mindset
- Humble
- Willingness to step back
- Genuine

- ◆ Engaged
- ◆ Intentional
- ◆ Consistent
- ◆ Knowledgeable (of child development, outdoor skills, and natural history)
- ◆ Playful
- ◆ Embraces wonderment
- ◆ Inclusive (cultural responsiveness/tolerance/diversity/ acceptance)

Exploring the character aspects educator roles

In the following, we have noted characteristics that we've noticed make a difference in the engagement and flourishing of children. We've noted how these characteristics connect to the various roles we've discussed in previous chapters.

We encourage you to take your time with each of these characteristics to deeply and realistically explore how these characteristics present themselves in you during a day. In which moments are you more or less aligned with this characteristic? How might you shift your own thinking or behavior to be more aligned?

We also invite you to think critically about the characteristics we've suggested. Do you agree these are vital for adults who care for children? Are there other characteristics you would add?

As you reflect, please be gentle with yourself. This isn't a time to "should on yourself," where you say things like, "I should be more XYZ," or "I should know better." Rather, we're inviting you to be curious about yourself while also caring for yourself, so you can be confident you are supporting children in the best way possible at this moment. Remember, we're striving for life-long learning where we are constantly growing.

Self-aware

In order to care for others, we need to care for ourselves first. We rarely hold a mirror to ourselves but rather focus on practice. We believe the two aspects are intertwined. That is, what you create is a result of the relationship between yourself as an adult, the place in which you work, and the children with whom you work. Understanding our own pedagogical principles, our weaknesses, our strengths, our personal biases, and so forth allows us to move forward in continuous improvement. If adults are self-aware, we can create teams of effective educators with multiple strengths who work together collectively to offer experiences and opportunities that support children to not just develop but also flourish.

Self-awareness, of course, requires self-reflection. It is useful to regularly take a block of time to push ourselves to think about our own attitudes and behaviors and how those integrate with teaching practice. A few self-reflections to consider include the following:

- ◆ To what extent did I engage children through my experiences, skills, and knowledge this week?
- ◆ Look at the weekly plans and ask, how did my attitudes and fears affect my choice of experience? Was there an emphasis on certain learning domains areas such as art, math, and so on? Was there an emphasis on a particular location?
- ◆ What richness did I bring to learning moments today?
- ◆ How do I view children?
- ◆ How do I view my co-workers?
- ◆ How do I view families?
- ◆ Record an interaction with children. What did I say? What was the tone? How did I position my body? Taken together, what message did that convey to children?
- ◆ Did I smile today?

Open to new ideas with a personal growth mindset

Self-awareness only goes so far in our interactions with other children, co-workers, and families. Once we're aware, we have to be open and willing to consider the way we're doing things is not the most effective approach. This is a growth mindset—the belief that we can always learn and improve (Dweck & Leggett, 1988).

In nature-based education, we never find ourselves in the same situation with children from one day to the next. It is this variability that engages adults by requiring constant review and analysis. For us, educating is a dynamic process that requires adults to be open to new ideas, possibilities, and changes in our own behaviors. These ideas come from colleagues and the children themselves. Wherever the ideas come from, educators must be willing to grow and evolve. This approach to professional growth and development enables adults to refine all the roles in this book. It embraces the fact that there is always something to consider, reflect on, and develop.

Humble

Being open to learning and growing means that sometimes we will need to reevaluate our approaches and thinking. Like it or not, sometimes as adults, we can be egocentric in our thinking. We have been on the planet longer than children obviously, but we don't know everything they know or see the world in the way they do. It is this acceptance of our human frailties and imperfections that co-construction develops a greater understanding for both parties–the child and the adult—that leads us to recognize humility as a vital teacher characteristic. Humility is particularly apparent in the sensitivity of facilitating experiences (Chapter 5) and the role of guide and mentor (Chapter 11). In the chapters on providers of space, resources, and time, the adult not only creates an effective environment that meets children's needs through observation but also listens to them in order to fine-tune and adjust. How they interact in that space as a guide and mentor affects the experiences in that environment. This requires humility.

Willingness to step back

Humility directly relates to educators' willingness to step back and allow children to lead. The co-constructivist approach requires the adult and the child to work together in a way that allows both to lead at different points of the journey. Allowing children to lead requires the adult to step back, give up a bit of control and power, and allow the child to feel a sense of ownership. This willingness to step back rather than lead the learning is essential for all child-centered learning—a core tenet of nature-based pedagogy. This willingness relates to all our roles explored in this book but particularly to the provider of time (Chapter 3) and in the facilitator of experiences (Chapter 5) as the pressure to lead can be related to the drive to get things done.

Genuine

Being genuine with children shares who we are and that we are interested to hear their ideas, theories, and reflections. When we look a child in the eye and really hear what they are saying it provides a feedback loop to say, "I value you and your thinking." It starts from birth and places children as significant, treasured beings. Being genuine is at the root of relationship building (Chapter 7), but it is also a characteristic that runs throughout all the roles we have defined in this book. When the adult has a genuine affection and admiration for children, it is demonstrated in everything they do.

Engaged

This characteristic requires an adult to be able to find the world around them interesting—to be curious as to why, how, and what if. To be able to find the simplest of things, such as jumping in a puddle, interesting. Being engaged with a child or a group of children draws on the ability to focus and concentrate whilst still being able to sense the space around you. We explore this in Chapter 9 on risk management, where the process of balancing engagement and supervision is explored.

Intentional—A thinker

When our actions are intentional it demonstrates that we have thoughtfully reflected on our practice. When the thinking process doesn't take place, programs are created that are haphazardly piecemealed. As a result, these programs miss the connection to children both in the content offered, the resources provided, and sometimes even in the design and use of space. Awareness is the first step to being intentional, but real intentionality also includes purposeful action. Every role discussed in this book requires intentionality to fully implement. For example, the role of holding memories and documenting learning (Chapter 6) requires intentional action to make the thinking process of children, families, and staff visible. Whether this is by using the Floorbook approach (Warden, 2012b) or some other means of documentation, the actions around documentation are intentional.

Consistent

In a world that is unpredictable, children often don't know who or what to trust, so they learn to not trust any of it. By being consistent in our actions and expectations, we become reliable and predictable to children—they know what to expect. One way to embody consistency is not only in the role of providing space (Chapter 2) and time (Chapter 3) but also in our relationships (Chapter 7) and the conversations we have with children (Chapter 8).

Knowledgeable

The amount we know, are aware of, or have experienced makes a difference in our conversations. When adults know about child development, aspects of natural history, their local community's history, and any other knowledge it has two key effects. The first is an adult's confidence to talk with children goes up. The security to feel that we are prepared by developing knowledge of a subject or situation increases openness to debate or questioning.

The second is considering where the inquiry might take them. That is, the adult's awareness of the possibilities of play, exploration, and conversation is increased. If the awareness is limited about a subject like birds, for example, then the adult might not be aware of how different species of birds weave, mold, and design nests in unique ways. In contrast, having awareness of weaverbirds, swallows' mud nests, and bowerbirds and their fascination with the color blue allows the adult to consider possible lines of development that children may find inspirational. The characteristic of seeking and having residual knowledge as the adult was explored in the chapters on providing time, space, resources, planning, and advocacy.

Playful

"Being playful in our hearts is a way to understand children." A colleague, Helle Nebelong, said this to Claire once when discussing landscape design. It is a different thing from playing with children and being in the play. We hold in our mind the effectiveness of the location, the relevance of context, and the purpose of resources as adults and consider if they lift a child's engagement and indeed our own inner sense of playfulness. The playful heart of the adult comes through in Chapter 5 as the facilitator of experiences as the awareness the adult has on the impact of ownership and joy in play and learning.

Embraces wonderment

When our days become repetitive without intentional mindfulness and gratitude, they lack luster. This can even happen in nature-based learning environments Inside, Outside, and Beyond. Great teachers hold onto a wonderment that allows our adult brain to still be amazed at the feats and features of the natural world. Consider your emotions when you watch a starfish walking along the beach, find a crisp leaf on an autumn day, watch a butterfly you haven't seen before, and observe a spider's web that shimmers like gold or maps a river carving meanders into the land. These moments provide a connection to something greater than ourselves and renew our own vitality and love of the world. If educators have a sense of wonder, they will pass it on to children in their tone of voices, the look on their faces, and even the way they learn to experience more of what they've seen. We explored these ideas in Chapter 8 on the art of being a conversationalist. This characteristic is explored as a moment of connection between the adult and the child in a joint experience, a conversation that often goes beyond words.

Inclusive

All children and their families should feel welcomed and wanted in a space, whether that is Inside, Outside, or Beyond the gate. In order to create this sense of belonging, adults need to respond and sustain children's cultures in order to embrace diversity.

Since we are constantly sending implicit and explicit messages to the world, adults need to be aware of their own biases and beliefs around inclusivity. A lack of awareness has great potential to alienate children and families, thus undermining effective teaching practices. Due to the nature of inclusivity, it is part of every role we play as educators. Inclusivity requires a constant awareness of the needs of the many provided by the few.

Your work matters

As we said earlier, our goal with this chapter was to encourage you to get curious about yourself so that you support children in the best way possible in any given moment. We appreciate the fact you're reading this book. That act alone inherently illustrates a growth mindset and willingness to keep learning. We are also incredibly grateful for the work you do every day to connect young children with nature and hope this book helps you think of ways to make the experience even better for both you and the children.

We opened the book with reminders of the heaviness of the world right now. While that heaviness remains and, in many ways, we have little control over those events, we do have the power to create a positive learning environment for young children. We do have the power to instill confidence, curiosity, and care in them to support their lives now and into the future. We hope you'll use this power for good to help children thrive learning with each other and the natural world.

References and resources

Agbenyega, J. S. (2012). How we view our theoretical competency: Early childhood pre-service teachers' self-evaluation of a professional placement experience. *Australian Journal of Early Childhood*, 37, 141–147. https://doi.org/10.1177/183693911203700219

Bailie, P. E., Larimore, R. A., & Pikus, A. E. (2023). *Evaluating natureness: Measuring the quality of nature-based classrooms in pre-K through 3rd grade*. Gryphon House.

Barnett, L., Beurden, E., Morgan, P., Brooks, L., & Beard, J. (2009). Childhood motor skill proficiency as a predictor of adolescent physical activity. *The Journal of Adolescent Health: Official Publication of the Society for Adolescent Medicine*, 44, 252–259. https://doi.org/10.1016/j.jadohealth.2008.07.004

Bench, S. W., & Lench, H. C. (2013). On the function of boredom. *Behavioral Sciences*, 3(3), 459–472. https://doi.org/10.3390/bs3030459

Brown, B. (2010, June). *The power of vulnerability* [Video]. TED Conferences. https://www.ted.com/talks/brene_brown_the_power_of_vulnerability

Brown, B. (2021). *Atlas of the heart: Mapping meaningful connection and the language of human experience*. Random House.

Broström, S. (2017). A dynamic learning concept in early years' education: a possible way to prevent schoolification. *International Journal of Early Years Education*, 25(1), 3–15. https://doi.org/10.1080/09669760.2016.1270196

Cabell, S. Q., Justice, L. M., McGinty, A. S., DeCoster, J., & Forston, L. D. (2015). Teacher-child conversations in preschool classrooms: Contributions to children's vocabulary development. *Early Childhood Research Quarterly*, 30(PA), 80–92. https://doi.org/10.1016/j.ecresq.2014.09.004

Cameron-Faulkner, T., Macdonald, R., Serratrice, L., Melville, J., & Gattis, M. (2017). Plant yourself where language blooms: Direct experience of nature changes how parents and children talk about nature. *Youth and Environments*, 27(2), 110–124. https://doi.org/10.7721/chilyoutenvi.27.2.0110

Casey, T. (2016). *Children's need for time and space in play. in Environments for Outdoor Play* (pp. 5–16). Sage Publications. Retrieved January 28, 2024 from https://www.sagepub.com/sites/default/files/upm-binaries/15553_CASEY_C01.PDF

Chawla, L., & Hart, R. A. (1995). The roots of environmental concern. *The NAMTA Journal*, 20(1), 148–157.

Chen, J. J., & de Groot, S. K. (2014). The quality of teachers' interactive conversations with preschool children from low-income families during small-group and large-group activities. *Early Years*, 34(3), 272–289. https://doi.org/10.1080/09575146.2014.912203

Collaborative for Spirituality in Education. (n.d.) Retrieved from https://spiritualityineducation.org/

Csikszentmihalyi, M. (1990). *Flow: the psychology of optimal experience.* Harper and Row.

D'Amore, C., & Chawla, L. (2018). Significant life experiences that connect children with nature: A research review and applications to a family nature club. In A. Cutter-Mackenzie, K. Malone, & E. Barratt Hacking (Eds.), *Research Handbook on Childhoodnature* (pp. 1–27). Springer. https://doi.org/10.1007/978-3-319-51949-4_49-1

De Rivera, C., Girolametto, L., Greenberg, J., & Weitzman, E. (2005). Children's responses to educators' questions in day care play groups. *American Journal of Speech-Language Pathology*, 14(1), 14–26. https://doi.org/10.1044/1058-0360(2005/004)

Dewey, J., & Boydston, J. A. (1988). *The later works of John Dewey, 1925-1953: 1938-1939, experience and education, freedom and culture, theory of valuation, and essays.* SIU Press.

Dickinson, D. K., Golinkoff, R. M., & Hirsh-Pasek, K. (2010). Speaking out for language: Why language is central to reading development. *Educational Researcher*, 39(4), 305–310. https://doi.org/10.3102/0013189X10370204

Dillard, A. (1989). *The writing life.* Harper Perennial.

Dooley, B. A., & Fitzgerald, A. (2012). *My world survey: National study of youth mental health in Ireland. Headstrong and UCD School of*

Psychology. ISBN 978-0-9572608-0-1-8. Retrieved January 25, 2024, from https://researchrepository.ucd.ie/entities/publication/f028b522-c3ed-4e3a-8ffe-e1578443f885/details; http://hdl.handle.net/10197/4286

Driver, R. (1983). *The pupil as scientist?* Open University Press.

Duckworth, E. (1987). *"The Having of Wonderful Ideas" & other essays on teaching & learning*. Teachers College Press.

Dweck, C. S., & Leggett, E. (1988). A social-cognitive approach to motivation and personality. *Psychological Review*, 95(2), 256–273. https://doi.org/10.1037/0033-295X.95.2.256

Forsyth, D. R. (2024). The psychology of groups. In R. Biswas-Diener, & E. Diener (Eds.), *Noba textbook series: Psychology*. DEF publishers. Retrieved January 28, 2024, from http://noba.to/trfxbkhm

Fox, H., Gessler, M., Higgins, A., Meade, A., Warden, C., & Williams-Ridge, S. (2021). *Environmental Kinship Framework*. Retrieved December 20, 2021, from www.environmentalkinship.org

Gill, T. (2007). *No fear: Growing up in a risk averse society*. Calouste Gulbenkian Foundation.

The Gottman Institute: A Research Based Approach to Relationships. (n.d.) Retrieved from https://www.gottman.com/

Grant, A. (2021). *Think again: The power of knowing what you don't know*. Viking.

Gray, P. (2008). *The value of play I: The definition of play gives insights*. Retrieved from http://www.psychologytoday.com/blog/freedom-learn/200811/the-value-play-i-the-definition-play-gives-insights

Gray, P. (2013). *Definitions of play. Scholarpedia*, 8(7), 30578. https://doi.org/10.4249/scholarpedia.30578

Hannust, T., & Kikas, E. (2010). Young children's acquisition of knowledge about the Earth: A longitudinal study. *Journal of Experimental Child Psychology*, 107, 164–180.

Hanscom, A. (2016). *Balanced and barefoot*. New Harbinger Publications.

Hart, T. (2005). Spiritual experiences and capacities of children and youth. *Handbook of spiritual development in childhood and adolescence* (pp. 163–178). Sage.

Hedderson, M. M., Bekelman, T. A., Li, M., Knapp, E. A., Palmore, M., Dong, Y., Elliott, A. J., Friedman, C., Galarce, M., Gilbert-Diamond, D.,

Glueck, D., Hockett, C. W., Lucchini, M., McDonald, J., Sauder, K., Zhu, Y., Karagas, M. R., Dabelea, D., & Ferrara, A. (2023). Trends in screen time use among children during the COVID-19 pandemic, July 2019 through August 2021. *JAMA Network Open*, 6(2), E2256157. https://doi.org/10.1001/jamanetworkopen.2022.56157

Hughes, B. (2011). *Evolutionary playwork* (2nd ed.). Routledge.

Kashdan, T. B., Gallagher, M. W., Silvia, P. J., Winterstein, B. P., Breen, W. E., Terhar, D., & Steger, M. F. (2009). The curiosity and exploration inventory-II: Development, factor structure, and psycho-metrics. *Journal of Research in Personality*, 43, 987–998.

Keltner, D. (2023). *Awe: The new science of everyday wonder and how it can transform your life*. Penguin Press.

Kets de Vries, M. F. (2014). Doing nothing and nothing to do: The hidden value of empty time and boredom. *Organizational Dynamics*, 44(3), 169–175.

Larimore, R. A. (2011). *Establishing a nature-based preschool*. National Association for Interpretation.

Larimore, R. A. (2016). Defining nature-based preschools. *International Journal of Early Childhood Environmental Education*, 4(1), 33–37.

Larimore, R. A. (2018). Using principles of nature-based preschools to transform your classroom. *Young Children*, 73(11), 34–41.

Larimore, R. A. (2019). *Preschool beyond walls: Blending early childhood education and nature-based learning*. Gryphon House.

Larimore, R. A. (2021). *Investigating teacher-child interactions in a nature-based and non-nature preschool*. Michigan State University.

Leuchter, M., Saalbach, H., Studhalter, U., Tettenborn, A., Leuchter, M., Saalbach, H., Studhalter, U., & Tettenborn, A. (2020). Teaching for conceptual change in preschool science: Relations among teachers' professional beliefs, knowledge, and instructional practice. *International Journal of Science Education*, 42(12), 1–27. https://doi.org/10.1080/09500693.2020.1805137

Louv, R. (2005) *Last child in the woods :saving our children from nature-deficit disorder*. Algonquin Books.

Massey, S. L., Pence, K. L., Justice, L. M., & Bowles, R. P. (2008). Educators' use of cognitively challenging questions in economically disadvantaged preschool classroom contexts. *Early Education and Development*, 19(2), 340–360. https://doi.org/10.1080/10409280801964119

Mayer, J. D., Salovey, P., & Caruso, D. R. (2000). Models of emotional intelligence. In R. J. Sternberg (Ed.), *Handbook of intelligence* (pp. 396–420). Cambridge University Press.

Mellers, B., Fincher, K., Drummond, C., & Bigony, M. (2013). Surprise. A belief or an emotion? In *Progress in brain research* (1st ed., Vol. 202). Elsevier B.V. https://doi.org/10.1016/B978-0-444-62604-2.00001-0

Miller, L. (2015). *The spiritual child: The new science on parenting for health and lifelong thriving*. Picador.

Mlodinow, L. (2022). *Emotional: How feelings shape our thinking*. Knopf Doubleday Publishing Group.

Murray, C. G. (2021). *Illuminating care: The pedagogy and practice of care in early childhood communities*. Exchange Press.

National Education Scotland the One Good Adult Job Description Implementation Guidance. Retrieved January 25, 2024, from https://www.gov.scot/publications/cypmhw-joint-delivery-board-newsletter-july-2022/pages/4/

Nedo, N. (2020). *The organic artist for kids: A DIY guide to making your own eco-friendly art supplies from nature*. Quarto.

Nicholson, S. (1971). Theory of loose parts: How not to cheat children. In *Landscape architecture* (Vol. 62, pp. 30–34).

Nunes, T. (1995) Cultural practices and the conception of individual differences: Theoretical and empirical considerations. *New Directions for Child and Adolescent Development Journal* 95(67), 91–103.

Oswald, T. K., Rumbold, A. R., Kedzior, S. G. E., & Moore, V. M. (2020). Psychological impacts of "screen time" and "green time" for children and adolescents: A systematic scoping review. *PLoS ONE*, 15(9), 1–52. https://doi.org/10.1371/journal.pone.0237725

Paley, V. G. (1981). *Wally's stories*. Harvard University Press.

Piff, P. K., Toronto, M. F., Dietze, P., Keltner, D. M., & Dacher, S. (2015). Awe, the small self, and prosocial behavior. *Journal of Personality and Social Psychology*, 108(6), 883–899.

Prins, J., van der Wilt, F., van Santen, S., van der Veen, C., & Hovinga, D. (2023). The importance of play in natural environments for children's language development: An explorative study in early childhood education. *International Journal of Early Years Education*, 31(2), 450–466. https://doi.org/10.1080/09669760.2022.2144147

Realising the ambition. (2020). Education Scotland, Scottish Government. Retrieved January 27, 2024, from https://education.gov.scot/improvement/learning-resources/realising-the-ambition/; https://thereggioapproach.weebly.com/reggio-philosophy-and-principles.html

Reigeluth, C. M., & Carr-Chellman, A. A. (Eds.). (2009). *Instructional-design theories and models, volume III: Building a common knowledge base* (1st ed.). Routledge. https://doi.org/10.4324/9780203872130

Rideout, V. J., Foehr, U. G., & Roberts, D. F. (2010). *Generation M2: Media in the lives of 8- to 18-year-olds (Report #8010).* Kaiser Family Foundation.

Robson, S. (2006). *Developing thinking and understanding in young children* (2nd ed.). Routledge.

Sandseter, E. B. H. (2009). Characteristics of risky play. *Journal of Adventure Education & Outdoor Learning*, 9(March), 3–21. https://doi.org/10.1080/14729670802702762

Schaefer, L. (2022). The influence of significant life experiences on the teaching practices of early childhood educators in traditional and nature-based preschools. *International Journal of Early Childhood Environmental Education*, 9(3), 39–48.

Schein, D. (2014). Nature's role in children's spiritual development. *Children, Youth and Environments*, 24(2), 78–101. https://doi.org/10.7721/chilyoutenvi.24.2.0078

Schein, D. (2018). *Inspiring wonder, awe, and empathy: Spiritual development in young children.* Redleaf Press.

Sims Bishop, R. (1990). Mirrors, windows, and sliding glass doors. *Perspectives: Choosing and Using Books for the Classroom*, 6(3), ix–xi.

Siraj-Blatchford, I. (2009). Conceptualising progression in the pedagogy of play and sustained shared thinking in early childhood education: a Vygotskian perspective. *Education and Child Psychology*, 26(2), 77–89.

Sylva, K., Melhuish, E., Sammons, P., Siraj-Blatchford, I., & Taggart, B. (2004). *The Effective Provision of Pre-School Education (EPPE) project.* Retrieved January 25, 2024.

Tamokoshi, S., Shimai, S., Sogo, S., & Yagi, A. (2011). The psychophysiological effects of the fireplace. *Pyschologia*, 54, 68–79.

Thiery, W., Lange, S., Rogel, J., Schleussner, C. F., et al. (2021). Intergenerational inequities in exposure to climate extremes: Young generations are severely threatened by climate change. *Science*, 374(6564), 158–160.

Tolle, E. (2004). *A new Earth: Awakening to your life's purpose*. Penguin.

Tu, T.-H., & Hsiao, W.-Y. (2008). Preschool teacher-child verbal interactions in science teaching. *Electronic Journal of Science Education*, 12(2), 199–223.

UNICEF. (1989). *Convention on the Rights of the Child*. Retrieved from www.unicef.org/crc

Valanides, N. Gritsi, F. Kampeza, M., & Ravanis, K. (2000). Changing pre-school children's conceptions of the day/night cycle. *International Journal of Early Years Education*, 8(1), 27–39. https://doi.org/10.1080/096697600111725

Vygotsky, L. (1986). *Thought and language*. MIT Press.

Wadsworth, P. (1997). Document 9: Children's ideas in science. In P. Murphy (Ed.), *Making sense of science study guide*. SPE/Open University.

Waller, T. (2011). Adults are essential: The roles of adults outdoors. In J. White (Ed.), *Outdoor provision in the early years*. Sage Publications.

Waltzer, K., Kärkkäinen, S., & Havu-Nuutinen, S. (2023). Early childhood professionals' pedagogical decision making. *International Journal of Early Years Education*. https://doi.org/10.1080/09669760.2023.2261496

Warden, C. (2007). *Learning pathways*. Mindstretchers Ltd.

Warden, C. (2012a). *Nature kindergartens and forest schools* (2nd ed.). Mindstretchers Ltd.

Warden, C. (2012b). *Talking and thinking floorbooks* (2nd ed.). Mindstretchers Ltd.

Warden, C. (2015). *Learning with nature: Embedding outdoor practice*. Sage Publications.

Warden, C. (2019). Nature pedagogy: The art of being with nature inside, outside and beyond. *Pedagogy Magazine*, 34(6). Liverpool Hope University.

Warden, C. (2020). *Planning with and for children – A practical guide to inquiry-based learning through Floorbooks*. Essential Resources. ISBN: 9781925145434

Warden, C. (2022). *Green teaching: Nature pedagogies for climate change and sustainability*. Corwin.

Warden, C., & Fargher, D. (Eds.). (2023). *Beyond the gate: Respecting the relationship of children, culture and the natural world*. Pademelon Press. ISBN: 9781876138639

White, J. (2002). *The child's mind*. Routledge Falmer.

Willig, J. (1990). *Children's concepts and the primary curriculum*. Paul Chapman.

Wilson, R. (2012). *Nature and young children: Encouraging creative play and learning in natural environments*. Routledge.

Glossary of terms

Beyond   the area beyond the boundaries of the designated outdoor play area (i.e., Outside), which or may not be fenced. This is one of the three spaces of nature pedagogy—the Inside, the Outside, and the Beyond

Breadth   engaging children in a greater range of experiences, using a wider range of contexts for learning

Challenge and enjoyment   enabling children to be engaged, take responsibility, solve problems, and lead and develop further their passion for learning

Classroom   where a group of children and adults interact and function as a group within an early learning setting. The Inside, Outside, and Beyond spaces all serve as classroom spaces

Coherence   helping children to make connections in their learning, using real life contexts that help children make sense of and apply their learning

Depth   deepening children's understandings, taking children further and deeper in their inquiry

Educator   the adult responsible for the care, nurturing, and development of children. This is used interchangeably with *teacher* and adult throughout the book

Floorbook™   a group documentation and planning strategy that develops both adult created curricula and an emergent curriculum

Inside   refers to the space inside a built structure. This is often a permanent structure like a building but could be semi-permanent like a yurt. This is one of the three spaces of nature pedagogy—the Inside, the Outside, and the Beyond

Nature pedagogy or nature-based pedagogy   a way of working with children that acknowledges our interrelationship with the natural world by providing opportunities for children to learn *with* nature for the health of individual children, communities, and the planet

Outside   the designated outdoor play area. This is one of the three spaces of nature pedagogy—the Inside, the Outside, and the Beyond

Outdoors   collective term for being in a space separate from the indoor space. This could include both Outside and Beyond spaces

Personalization and choice   tailoring provision to meet individual needs and interests, supporting children to make choices and share their perspectives

Place-based   connected to local community, culture, and the natural environment

Progression   building on what children know already, providing provocations and stimulations to extend learning

Provocation   a material or interaction that initiates, deepens, or seeks to engage children in something they may not be aware of or familiar with

Relevance   connecting with the children's needs and interests, reflecting children's lives, interests, and culture

Talking Tub   a collection of images and objects designed to support consultation with children and support Floorbook™ planning

Teacher   the adult responsible for the care, nurturing, and development of children. This is used interchangeably with educator and adult throughout the book

For Product Safety Concerns and Information please contact our EU
representative GPSR@taylorandfrancis.com Taylor & Francis Verlag GmbH,
Kaufingerstraße 24, 80331 München, Germany

Printed and bound by CPI Group (UK) Ltd, Croydon, CR0 4YY
08/06/2025
01896999-0011